THE   LUT   D

The Law of Copyright

&

Rights in Performances

Second Edition

DENIS DE FREITAS

Honorary President of The British Copyright Council

Published by The British Copyright Council
29/33 Berners Street, London W1P 4AA

First Edition © 1990 Denis de Freitas
ISBN 0 901 73705 4

Second Edition © 1998 Denis de Freitas
ISBN 0 901 73707 0

Printed in England by Halstan & Co Ltd

The Law of Copyright and Rights in Performances

SECTION II – RIGHTS IN PERFORMANCES

Background

SECTION III - FINAL OBSERVATIONS

APPENDICES   **Pages**

INTRODUCTION

Historical Background and Purpose of Copyright

1.1   Throughout recorded history human societies have recognised the importance to the community of the talents of their writers, composers and artists, but until the development of the copyright system these gifted and indispensable members of society were supported principally by patronage – of the royal courts, the aristocracy, the great guilds and the churches; and those without patronage, or adequate patronage, had to support themselves by working in other occupations. Shakespeare supported himself not as a playwright but as an actor/manager.

1.2   There is still room for patronage today, by the Government and by the private sector, to support certain categories of cultural and artistic endeavour which are not adequately supported by the copyright system; but these are special cases. The copyright system has by now become an essential component of the infrastructure of modern society, enabling creative people and those who are engaged in the business of disseminating their works, by their creative talents on the one hand and by entrepreneurial skills on the other, to earn a living for themselves, free from dependence upon patronage.

1.3   The object of the copyright system, therefore, is to encourage authors to write, musicians to compose, and artists to paint; and to provide incentives for the public presentation and distribution of their works on as wide a scale as possible. Copyright is often described as the trading system for works of the mind, whether they are expressed in some tangible form, such as a book, a painting or a recording of music, or captured, in analogue or digital format, in an electronic storage device; although the works themselves – the words, the colours and patterns, the sounds – are intangible. The copyright system achieves this object by giving authors, composers, and other creative people rights of control over the various ways in which the public make use of their works.

1.4   There is a tendency for the subject of copyright to be regarded as an esoteric branch of law concerned exclusively with a small sector of society – the authors, composers, artists, performers and their business partners the publishers, record companies and film producers. This is, however, a complete misconception. The copyright system is a vital part of modern society serving the entire community. It is the foundation on which the world's publishing industry rests, bringing the written or recorded word, carrying knowledge, ideas, understanding and entertainment to every literate person, young or old. On it depend the vast national and international networks of distribution and supply which service a country's educational institutions. The orderly acquisition and transfer of rights which take place within the copyright system are indispensable to the entire media – newspapers, journals, radio and television; and, of course, the whole world of entertainment – theatres, concerts, films, broadcasting and record production – depends upon a regular supply of literary, dramatic, musical and artistic works, the creation and dissemination of which is stimulated and regulated by the copyright system. Moreover, with the extension of the system to the protection of computer software, much of the industrial and commercial activity of the country involves the use of rights established by copyright.

The Sources of the Law

2.1 The law of copyright and the related field, rights in performances, is contained in a code of statutory provisions, as interpreted from time to time by judicial decisions. The first copyright statute in the world was the UK Statute of Anne 1709. The present statutory code is contained in the Copyright, Designs and Patents Act 1988 which came into force on 1 August 1989; and in various statutory instruments made under the Act. The provisions dealing with copyright are in Part I of the Act comprising 204 sections, and in 7 sections in Part VII (ss.296-299); the law relating to rights in performances is in Part II comprising 54 sections and in Schedule 2A; and Schedules 1 and 2 contain a code of transitional and other provisions.

2.2 Since its commencement on 1 August 1989 the 1988 Act has been substantially amended, particularly in order to implement various European Union Directives. Appendix 1 lists the principal laws (both statutes and subsidiary legislation) by which the 1988 Act has been amended. The Appendix also lists the relevant Directives and the Regulations by which they have been implemented. Subsidiary legislation made under the 1988 Act (other than the regulations implementing the Directives), which is very numerous and voluminous, has not been included in the Appendix. The Appendix represents the position as at 31 December 1997.

2.3 This Guide does not purport to cover every provision contained in the legislation; moreover, many of the provisions were new and are not yet the subject of established and accepted practices or judicial interpretation, so that their full effect may be uncertain.

2.4   The Guide seeks to present the essential features of the law; it is a highly specialised field and anyone with an apparent problem carrying significant financial implications should obtain professional advice.

SECTION I - COPYRIGHT

Nature of Copyright

3.   Copyright is a form of property, and arises automatically on the creation of various categories of works, provided that in the case of literary, dramatic and musical works the work has been recorded in writing or some other format, which would include storage in a computer memory – see para. 6.3 below.

Territorial Application of the Law

4.1   Part I of the 1988 Act (relating to copyright) applies to anything done in –

     (a) England, Wales, Scotland and Northern Ireland;
     (b) the territorial waters of the United Kingdom, and the UK sector of the continental shelf;
     (c) ships, aircraft and hovercraft registered in the United Kingdom (ss.157(1), 161, 162)

4.2   Part I may also, by Order in Council –
     (a) be extended to
          (i)   any of the Channel Islands,
          (ii) the Isle of Man,
          (iii) any colony;
     (b) be applied to any foreign country.
          (ss.157(2), 159)

4.3   Appendix 2 contains lists of the overseas territories and other countries to which the copyright law of the United Kingdom has been extended or applied. It should be noted that in the case of some Commonwealth territories the UK law which is in force in the territory may not be the 1988 Act, but may be the 1956 Act or even the earlier 1911 Act.

4.4   One implication of the extension or application of UK law to an overseas territory or another country is that works originating in the United Kingdom will normally be protected in that territory or country; but there are some exceptions.

What Works are Protected by Copyright

5.1   The Act contains descriptions of three broad categories of works which are protected, viz –

(a) literary, dramatic, musical and artistic works,
(b) sound recordings, films, broadcasts and cable programmes,
(c) the typographical arrangements of published editions. (s.1(1))

5.2   These descriptions cover a very wide range of works; the following list is not necessarily comprehensive but will indicate the ambit of the three categories.

5.3   Literary and dramatic works
These include not only books, pamphlets, plays, articles for magazines, but virtually every form of written communication, including tables, compilations and databases; for example the script for a film or a programme for radio or television, a computer program (including preparatory design material for a program), a list of football fixtures, the text of a TV commercial, even private correspondence, are all within this category. (s.3(1))

5.4   Titles, names, ideas
Copyright does not protect the title of a book or play, nor a name as such, even if the name has been specially devised for a particular purpose. Nor does copyright protect an idea as such, but if the idea is recorded in written or other form, then the description of the idea contained in that record will be protected and may not be used, save with the permission of the author or other copyright owner. The recipes in a cookery book may be used freely, but the instructions in each recipe may not be copied and published by someone else without the copyright owner's permission.

5.5   Musical works
These include every form of musical composition from symphonies to advertising jingles. (s.3(1))

5.6   Artistic works
This is a large class covering paintings, drawings, photographs, engravings, sculptures, architectural works, maps and charts and includes the drawings for typefaces and for industrial designs, such as drawings for household furniture or a piece of machinery. It also includes works of artistic craftsmanship e.g. pottery or wooden carvings. It should be noted that a single frame of a movie film is not, for copyright purposes, a photograph. (s.4)

5

5.7   Sound recordings
These include recordings of all kinds of sound including, for example, a topical interview, the song of a bird or a hurricane in full blast, and cover recordings whether made as discs, tapes or in any other form.

5.8   It should be noted that under the 1988 Act the soundtrack of a film was a sound recording in which copyright might subsist quite separate and distinct from the copyright in the film. (s.5(1) before amendment) With effect from 1 January 1997 the law was amended. The soundtrack accompanying a film is now treated as part of the film; any restricted act in relation to a film which involves also the sound track is an infringement, if unauthorised, only of the copyright in the film and not also of a separate copyright in the soundtrack. (s.5B(2)(3)) But if the recorded sounds which constitute the soundtrack are used separately from the film, copyright subsists in the recording and if the use is a restricted act the permission of the owner of the copyright in the recording is required. (s.5B(5))

5.9   Films
A film is defined as a recording on any medium from which a moving image may by any means be produced; it includes every kind of carrier of visual images which can be utilised to present moving pictures, whether by means of a film projector, transmission by television or showing on a television screen through a video player. (s.5B(1))

5.10   Broadcasts
The actual programme as transmitted by a radio or television broadcast is protected by copyright as an entity quite separate and distinct from the components, such as the script or the music, which may be incorporated in the programme. A broadcast includes an encrypted programme provided decoding equipment is lawfully available to the public. (s.6(1)(2))

5.11   Cable programmes
As in the case of a broadcast, the actual programme as transmitted in a cable service is protected separately from any copyright material in the programme; provided, however, the cable programme is not simply the immediate unchanged retransmission of a broadcast programme.(s.7(6)(a))

5.12   Typographical arrangements

These are not the same as typefaces; a typographical arrangement is the whole layout of the printed pages of a published edition of literary, dramatic or musical works (but not artistic works). (s.8)

5.13   Computer-generated works

This is a new category introduced by the 1988 Act which defines it as a work generated by computer in circumstances such that there is no human author of it. It probably refers to such productions as an updated version of a directory automatically produced by standing computer programs; but it is difficult to envisage the computer generation of a work without some human authorship; the standing program for producing the updated directory would have been written by a human programmer. (s.178)

Conditions for Protection

6.1   A work within one of the categories eligible for protection will only enjoy copyright if it fulfills certain conditions. The conditions vary depending on the category; the essential ones are summarised below.

6.2   A literary, dramatic, musical or artistic work must be original. This does not mean that it must be novel; it simply means that it must be the original work of the author and must not have been copied from someone else's work. In theory, if two people, each unknown to the other, produce identical works, each will enjoy copyright. (s.1(1)(a))

6.3   A literary, dramatic or musical work must be recorded (whether with or without the permission of the author), in writing or otherwise; and this includes any form of notation or code regardless of the method by which or the medium in or on which the work is recorded. (s.3(2)(3))

6.4   A database must be a collection of independent works, data or other material which –

(a) are arranged in a systematic or methodical way, and

(b) are independently accessible by electronic or other means.

A database will only be treated as original (and hence eligible for protection as a literary work) if, by reason of the selection or arrangement of its contents the database constitutes the author's own intellectual creation. (s.3A)

6.5   A broadcast –
        (a) must
                (i) be capable of being lawfully received by members of the public;
                     but the public may be in any country of the world; or
                (ii) have been transmitted for presentation to the public; thus, a
                     broadcast intended as an entirely private communication between
                     two individual persons would not be eligible for protection;
        (b) is not eligible for protection if it infringes the copyright in another
             broadcast or a cable programme. (s.6(1)(6))

6.6   A broadcast, including one transmitted via satellite, is made from the
        place where the programme-carrying signals are introduced into an
        uninterrupted chain of communication under the control and
        responsibility of the person making the broadcast, which in the case of
        a satellite transmission includes the chain up to the satellite and down
        to the earth. (s.6(4))

6.7   Where the place from which a broadcast via satellite is made is located
        in a country other than an EEA State, and the law of that country fails
        to provide at least –
        (a) exclusive broadcasting rights for the authors of literary, dramatic,
            musical and artistic works, films and broadcasts;
        (b) a right to consent for performers in respect of the live broadcast of
            their performances; and
        (c) a right for performers and producers of sound recordings to share
            equitable remuneration in respect of the broadcasting of their sound
            recordings;
        then –
        (i) if the place from which the programme–carrying signals are
             transmitted to the satellite is in an EEA State, that place is treated as
             the place from which the broadcast is made and the person operating
             the up–link station is treated as the person making the broadcast;
        (ii) if the up-link station is not in an EEA State but a person who is
             established in an EEA State has commissioned the making of the
             broadcast, that person is treated as the person making the broadcast,
             and the place where he has his principal establishment in the EEA
             is treated as the place from which the broadcast is made. (s.6A)

6.8 A broadcast transmitted in encrypted form would not be lawfully received unless the members of the public who receive it possess decoding equipment made available with the authority of the person who made the transmission or who provided the transmitted programme. (s.6(2))

6.9 A cable programme is not eligible for protection if it infringes the copyright in another cable programme or in a broadcast; nor is it covered by the Act if it falls into any of a long list of exempt categories (principally, operations which do not effectively serve the public). (s.7)

6.10 A work will only qualify for protection if –
(a) in the case of all works, the author was a qualifying person, (ss.153(1)(a), 154)
or
(b) in the case of all works except broadcasts and cable programmes, the work was first published in the United Kingdom, (ss.153(1)(b), 155)
and
(c) in the case of broadcasts and cable programmes, the work was made or sent from a place in the United Kingdom. (ss.153(1)(c),156)

6.11 A qualifying person is defined at some length in the Act but generally means any of the classes of British citizen, subject or protected person under the British Nationality Act 1981, or a person domiciled or resident in the United Kingdom, or a body incorporated under the law of the United Kingdom. (s.154)

6.12 Because the United Kingdom belongs to various conventions relating to copyright and related rights, protection under the Act has been applied to works whose authors are nationals or residents of countries which are members of those conventions or which have been first published in those countries. (s.159) Appendix 3 contains a list of the conventions of which the United Kingdom is a member.

6.13 First publication for copyright purposes has a special extended meaning; it includes any publication within 30 days of the actual first publication. (s.155(3))

6.14   Publication means the issue to the public of copies of works including, in the case of a literary, dramatic or musical work, making the work available by means of an electronic retrieval system; but it should be noted that the following acts are not treated as publication for the purposes of UK copyright law (otherwise than in relation to the publication right – see para. 9.15 below) –

(a) the public performance of a literary, dramatic or musical work, or of a sound recording or film;

(b) the broadcasting or cable distribution of a literary, dramatic, musical or artistic work, or of a sound recording or film;

(c) the issue to the public of copies of an artistic work, or of a film containing it. (s.175) (NB. Compare the wider meaning given to "release" – see para. 7.5(b) below)

Duration of Copyright

7.1   On 1 January 1996 the law relating to the duration of copyright and rights in performances was substantially changed to give effect to the EU Directive 93/98 EEC harmonizing the term of copyright and related rights. Under the amended law the periods during which copyright subsists in various categories of works are as follows:-

7.2   Literary, dramatic, musical and artistic works

Copyright expires 70 years after the end of the year in which author died. (s.12(2)) This general rule is subject to the following modifications –

7.2.1   Works of unknown authorship

(a) Copyright expires 70 years after the end of the year in which the work was made, or

(b) if it was made available to the public during that period, copyright expires 70 years after the end of the year in which it was made available; but

(c) if the identity of the author becomes known before either of the periods in paragraphs (a) or (b) has expired, the general rule will apply. (s.12(3)(4))

(d) "Making available" includes –

    (i) in the case of a literary, dramatic or musical work, performance in public, broadcast or inclusion in a cable programme service;

    (ii) in the case of an artistic work, exhibition in public, inclusion in a film which is shown in public, or in a broadcast or a cable programme service;

but no account may be taken of an unauthorised act. (s.12(5)).

7.2.2   Works originating in a non–EEA State
          If the author of a work which originated in a non-EEA State is not a
          national of an EEA State, the duration of copyright under the UK law
          will be the duration to which the work is entitled in its country of origin,
          but must not exceed the duration which would apply under s.12(2)-(5).
          (s.12(6))

7.2.3   Computer-generated works
          Copyright expires 50 years after the end of the year in which the work
          was made. (s.12(7))

7.2.4   Works of joint authorship
          For the purpose of applying the foregoing rules and modifications to a
          work of joint authorship –
          (i)   references to the death of the author mean the death of the last of
                the joint authors to die;
          (ii) where the identity of one or more, but not all, the joint authors is
                known, references to the death of the author mean the death of the
                last of the authors, whose identity is known, to die;
          (iii) references to the identity of the author becoming known mean the
                identity of any of the joint authors;
          (iv) references to the author not being a national of an EEA State mean
                none of the authors being an EEA national. (s.12(8))

7.2.5   EEA State
          An EEA State is a state which is a party to the Agreement on the
          European Economic Area signed at Oporto on 2 May 1992.

7.2.6   Exceptions
          Section 12 does not apply to Crown or Parliamentary copyright or to
          copyright vested in certain international organisations – see paragraphs
          7.3 and 7.4 below.

7.3   Crown copyright
          (a) Crown copyright in a literary, dramatic, musical or artistic work
              expires 125 years from the end of the year in which the work was
              made, or, if the work was published commercially within 75 years
              after it was made, then copyright expires 50 years after the end of
              the year in which it was so published. (s.163(3))

(b) Crown copyright in an Act of Parliament or Measure of the General Synod of the Church of England expires 50 years after the end of the year of the Royal Assent. (s.164(2))

7.4   Parliamentary copyright
(a) Parliamentary copyright in a literary, dramatic, musical or artistic work expires 50 years after the end of the year in which it was made.
(b) Copyright in a Parliamentary Bill expires on Royal Assent or on withdrawal or rejection at the end of the Session. (s.166(5))

7.5   Sound recordings
(a) The copyright in a sound recording expires –
    (i)   50 years after the end of the year in which it was made; or
    (ii) if released during that period, 50 years after the end of the year in which it was released. (s.13A(2))
(b) "Release" has a wide meaning including –
    (i)   first published (i.e. the first issue of copies to the public – see para. 6.14 above);
    (ii) first played in public;
    (iii) first broadcast;
    (iv) first included in a cable programme service;
provided in all cases that the act of release was authorised. (s.13A(3))
(c) Where the author of a sound recording is not a national of an EEA State, the duration is that to which the recording is entitled under the law of the country of which the author is a national, but must not exceed the duration which would apply under sub–paragraph (a) above, unless this restriction would be contrary to an international obligation entered into by the United Kingdom prior to 29 October 1993, in which case sub-paragraph (a) will apply. (s.13A(4)(5))

7.6   Films
(a) The copyright in a film expires –
    (i)   70 years after the end of the year in which the death occurs of the last of the following to die –
    the principal director,
    the author of the screenplay,
    the author of the dialogue,
    the composer of music specially composed for and used in the film; (s.13B(2)) but

(ii) where the identity of one or more, but not all, of the persons mentioned in sub-paragraph (i) is unknown, the reference to the death of the last means the death of the last whose identity is known; (s.13B(3))

(iii) where the identity of none of the persons mentioned in sub-paragraph (i) is known, the copyright expires 70 years after the end of the year in which the film was made, but if during that period the film was made available to the public, the copyright expires 70 years after the end of the year in which it was made available. (s.13B(4))

(b) "Making available to the public" includes showing in public, being broadcast and being included in a cable programme service, provided in all cases that the act of making available was authorised. (s.13B(6))

(c) Where neither the author, nor any of the joint authors, of a film which originated in a non-EEA State is a national of an EEA State the duration of copyright is that to which the film is entitled in the country of origin, but must not exceed the duration which would apply under sub–paragraph (a). (s.13B(7))

7.7   Broadcasts and cable programmes

(a) The copyright in a broadcast or cable programme expires 50 years after the end of the year in which the broadcast was made or the programme was included in a cable programme service, subject to sub–paragraph (b) following. (s.14(2))

(b) Where the author of a broadcast or cable programme is not a national of an EEA State, the duration is that to which the broadcast or programme is entitled in the country of which the author is a national, but must not exceed the duration which would apply under sub-paragraph (a) above, unless this restriction would be contrary to an international obligation entered into by the United Kingdom prior to 29 October 1993, in which case sub-paragraph (a) will apply. (s.14(3)(4))

7.8   Typographical arrangements

The copyright in a typographical arrangement expires 25 years after the end of the year in which the edition incorporating the arrangement was first published. (s.15)

7.9   Transition provisions relating to duration

7.9.1   In relation to works other than databases
(a) For the purposes of these provisions –
"existing" means made before 1 January 1996 (the date of the commencement of the Duration of Copyright and Rights in Performances Regulations 1995 (S.I. 1995 No. 3297) which amended the provisions in the 1988 Act relating to duration);
"existing copyright work" means a work in which copyright subsisted immediately before 1 January 1996. (Reg.14(1))
(b) Copyright in an existing copyright work continues to subsist until the date on which it would have expired under the 1988 Act if that date is later than the date on which it would expire under the amended law. (Reg. 15(1))
(c) The new duration provisions apply to –
(i)   copyright works made after 1 January 1996;
(ii) existing works which first qualify for protection after 1 January 1996; for example, preparatory design material for a computer program, which may not have been eligible for protection under the 1988 Act;
(iii) existing copyright works (subject to sub-paragraph (b) above);
(iv) existing works in which copyright under the 1956 or 1988 Acts had expired but which on 1 July 1995 were protected in another EEA State. For example, under the copyright law of Germany the general rule was, and is, that copyright expires 70 years after end of the year in which the author dies. By virtue of Article 7(1) of the Treaty of Rome, which prohibits "any discrimination on grounds of nationality" authors who are nationals of other EU States are entitled in Germany to the benefit of the life plus 70 duration even if in the country of origin the duration is a shorter period. Accordingly the copyright in a work by a UK author who died on, say, 1 July 1930 would have expired in the UK on 31 December 1980, but in Germany the work would be protected until 31 December 2000, and therefore under this transition provision copyright in the UK would revive on 1 January 1996 and continue until 31 December 2000.
(Reg.16)

7.9.2   In relation to databases

(a) When a database was created on or before 27 March 1996 and was protected by copyright on 31 December 1997, that copyright continues to subsist for the remainder of the duration applicable to literary works under s.12 of the Act.

(b) When the making of a database was completed on or after 1 January 1983, and database right (see para. 9.16 below) only began to subsist on 1 January 1998, that right expires at the end of 15 years after the end of the year 1997. (Regs. 29 and 30 of the Copyright and Rights in Databases Regulations 1997)

7.10   <u>Country of origin</u>

For the purposes of duration the country of origin of a work is governed by the following rules. (s.15A)

(i) The country of origin of a work which is first published in a Berne Convention country and is not published elsewhere within 30 days of that first publication, is the Berne country.

(ii) The country of origin of a work published within 30 days in two or more countries only one of which is a Berne country, is the Berne country.

(iii)Where a work is published in two or more countries of which two or more are Berne countries, then –

(a) if any of those countries is an EEA State, the country of origin is that State;

(b) if none of the countries is an EEA State, the country of origin is the Berne country which grants the shorter period of protection.

(iv) Where a work is unpublished or is first published in a non-Berne country (and is not published within 30 days in a Berne country), the country of origin is –

(a) if the work is a film and the maker has his headquarters in, or is domiciled or resident in a Berne country, that country;

(b) if the work is a work of architecture constructed in a Berne country or an artistic work incorporated in a building or other structure situated in a Berne country, that country; (c) in any other case, the country of which the author is a national.

15

Authorship and Ownership of Copyright

Author

8.1   The general rule is that the author of a work is the person who created it (s.9(1)), i.e. the writer, the composer, the artist, the photographer or the programmer; but there are some special rules.

8.2   The author –
(a) of a sound recording, is the producer; (s.9(2)(aa))
(b) of a film, is the producer and the principal director; and a film is treated as a work of joint authorship unless the producer and principal director are the same person; (ss.9(2)(ab),10(1A))
(c) of a broadcast, is the person who is responsible for the content of the programme and who transmitted it or made the arrangements necessary for transmitting it; (ss.9(2)(b), 6(3))
(d) of a cable programme, is the person who provided the programme service in which the programme was included; (s.9(2)(c))
(e) of a typographical arrangement, is the publisher of the edition in which it was incorporated; (s.9(2)(d))
(f) of a literary, dramatic, musical or artistic work which is computer generated, is the person who undertook the arrangements necessary for creating the work. (s.9(3))

Owner

8.3   The general rule is that as soon as a work has been created the copyright which automatically subsists in it belongs to the author (s.11(1)); but there are some exceptions, thus:
(a) in the case of a literary, dramatic, musical or artistic work made by an employee in the course of his employment, the employer is the first owner of the copyright unless there is an agreement to the contrary (s.11(2)); i.e. the onus is on the employee to contract out of this provision if he wishes to retain the copyright;
(b) in the case of a work made by an officer or servant of the Crown in the course of his duties, Her Majesty is the first owner of the copyright; (ss.11(3), 163(1)(b))
(c) in the case of Acts of Parliament and Measures of the General Synod of the Church of England, Her Majesty is the owner of the copyright; (s.164)
(d) in the case of a work made by or under the direction or control of

the House of Commons or the House of Lords, or a Bill introduced into either House, the relevant House is the first owner of the copyright; (ss.11(3), 165(1)(b), 166(2)(3)(4))

(e) in the case of a literary, dramatic, musical or artistic work made by an international organisation to which the copyright provisions of the Act have been extended, the organisation is the first owner of the copyright. (ss.11(3), 168(1))

8.4 It is to be noted that in cases (b) - (e) no provision is made for contracting out, which is expressly permitted in the case of (a).

8.5 It is important to note that ownership of an article such as a document or a painting, does not confer ownership of the copyright in it unless the copyright has been expressly assigned; thus, a letter will normally belong to the recipient, but the copyright in it – as a literary work – will belong to the writer. However, in the special case of the manuscript of an unpublished work, or an article embodying an unpublished sound recording or film, which is left by will it is presumed, in the absence of evidence to the contrary, that any rights of copyright owned by the testator should pass also to the legatee. (s.93)

Ownership of extended and revived copyright

8.6 The changes in the duration of copyright which took effect on 1 January 1996 necessitated special rules to determine who should enjoy the benefit of the extended and revived protection. These rules are –

(a) The copyright for the extended duration vests in the person who, immediately before 1 January 1996, was the owner of the copyright; unless that person owned the copyright for a shorter period than the full duration under the pre-1996 law, in which case the copyright for the extended duration will vest in the person to whom the pre-1996 copyright will revert. (Reg.18)

(b) The copyright in a work whose pre-1996 protection had expired before 1 January 1996 vests in the person who owned the pre-1996 copyright immediately before it expired; but if the former owner had died, or in the case of a legal entity had ceased to exist, before 1 January 1996 the revived copyright vests –

(i) in the case of a film, in the principal director or his legal personal representatives (to administer as part of his estate);

(ii) in any other case, in the author or his personal legal representatives (to administer as part of his estate). (Reg.19)

The Economic Rights of Copyright Owners – The Primary Rights

9.1   Copyright in a work gives the copyright owner the exclusive right to do, or authorise others to do all, or some, of the following acts in relation to the work. These acts are –

(a) copying the work;
(b) issuing copies of it to the public;
(c) renting or lending copies to the public;
(d) performing, showing or playing the work in public;
(e) broadcasting it or including it in a cable programme service;
(f) adapting the work, or doing any of the acts in (a) - (e) above in relation to an adaptation of the work. (s.16(1))

Whether the copyright in a work includes all these restricted acts depends on the category of the work. Thus:

9.2   Copying
Copying a work is covered by the copyright in every description of work. (s.17(1))

9.3   In relation to a literary, dramatic, musical or artistic work copying means reproducing it in any material form; the copy may be handwritten, typed, printed, photocopied, or in the form of a recording; and copying includes storing it in any medium by electronic means. It is therefore an infringement to re–record a record or tape of a copyright musical work whether the record or tape has been bought, borrowed or received as a present – or stolen! It is an infringement to make copies of a play for the use of the cast or of the parts of a symphony for the use of the members of the orchestra unless, in each case, the permission of the copyright owner has first been obtained. (s.17(2))

9.4   In relation to an artistic work copying includes the making of a copy in three dimensions of a two dimensional work or a copy in two dimensions of a three dimensional work. (s.17(3))

9.5   Issuing copies to the public
Issuing copies of a work to the public is covered by the copyright in every description of work. (s.18(1))

9.6   It should be noted that, save in the case of a computer program, this right only applies to –
(a) the act of putting into circulation in the EEA copies not previously

put into circulation in the EEA by or with the consent of the copyright owner; or

(b) the act of putting into circulation outside the EEA copies not previously put into circulation in the EEA or elsewhere;

but does not apply to –

(i)   any subsequent distribution, sale, hiring or loan of copies previously put into circulation; or

(ii) any subsequent importation of such copies;

but (i) and (ii) do not affect the exercise of the rental and lending right (see paras.9.8 and 9.9 below) or the right to control the circulation within (including the importation into) the EEA of copies not previously circulated in the EEA with the consent of the copyright owner, pursuant to sub-paragraph (a) above.(s.18(2))

9.7   In the case of a computer program issuing copies to the public means the act of putting into circulation copies not previously put into circulation in the United Kingdom or any other member state of the European Union by or with the consent of the copyright owner. (s.18(3))

9.8   Rental and lending
The rental or lending of copies to the public is covered by the copyright in –

(a) literary, dramatic or musical works;

(b) artistic works other than works of architecture in the form of buildings or models for buildings, or works of applied art;

(c) films and sound recordings. (s.18A(1))

9.9   "Rental" means making a copy of the work available for use, on terms that it will or may be returned, for direct or indirect economic or commercial advantage.
"Lending" means making a copy of the work available for use on terms that it will or may be returned, otherwise than for direct or indirect economic or commercial advantage, through an establishment which is accessible to the public. (s.18A(2))
"Rental" and "lending" do not include, inter alia –

(a) making available for the purpose of public performance, playing or showing in public, broadcasting or inclusion in a cable programme service;

(b) making available for the purpose of exhibition in public; or

(c) making available for on-the-spot reference use.(s.18A(3))

9.10 **Performing, playing or showing in public**
Performing, showing or playing a work in public is covered by the copyright in every description of work except a typographical arrangement. (s.19(1)(3))

9.11 This restricted act has a wide meaning; any performance which does not take place in a domestic or quasi-domestic situation is a public performance, including performances in clubs, even members' clubs.

9.12 **Broadcasting and inclusion in a cable programme service**
Broadcasting a work or including it in a cable programme service is covered by the copyright in every description of work except a typographical arrangement. (s.20)

9.13 **Adaptation**
Making an adaptation of a work is covered by the copyright in a literary, dramatic or musical work. (s.21(1))

9.14 An adaptation is the conversion of a non-dramatic work, such as a novel, into a dramatic work, such as a play, or vice versa; or a translation of it; or a version in which the story or action is presented mainly by pictures, e.g. a strip cartoon; and in the case of a musical work, an arrangement or transcription of it would be an adaptation. It would also be an adaptation to convert computer software written in one computer language into another computer language; or to arrange, make an unaltered version of, or translate a database. (s.21(3)(4))

9.15 **Publication right**
With effect from 1 December 1996 the 1988 Act was amended by the Copyright and Related Rights Regulations 1996 (S.I.1996 No.2967). One of the changes made was the establishment of a new property right, equivalent to copyright, to be known as "the publication right". The principal features of this new right are set out in the following subparagraphs.

9.15.1 Where the copyright in a literary, dramatic, musical or artistic work or a film has expired, and the work or film has never been published, a person who for the first time publishes the work or film, becomes entitled to the right, subject to certain conditions –
(i) the first publication must take place in the EEA;

(ii) the publisher, or in the case of a joint publication one of them, must be at the time of publication, a national of an EEA State;

(iii) publication must be authorised by the owner of the physical object in which the work or film is recorded.

9.15.2   The publication right comprises –
(i)   issuing copies to the public;
(ii) making available by means of an electronic retrieval system;
(iii) rental or lending to the public;
(iv) performing, exhibiting or showing in public;
(v) broadcasting or inclusion in a cable programme service;

9.15.3   The right does not arise from the publication of a work in which Crown or Parliamentary copyright had subsisted.

9.15.4   The right expires 25 years after the end of the year in which the work was first published. (Reg.16)

9.15.5   With certain exceptions, the substantive provisions of Part 1 of the 1988 Act (which deals with copyright), other than those relating to moral rights, apply mutatis mutandis to the publication right. (Reg.17)

9.16   Database right
With effect from 1 January 1998 the 1998 Act was amended by the Copyright and Rights in Databases Regulations 1997 to implement the EU Directive of 11 March 1996 on the legal protection of databases. One of the amendments was the establishment of a new database right. The principal features of this new right are set out in the following sub-paragraphs.

9.16.1   First owner of database right
The maker of a qualifying database is the first owner of the database right in it (Reg.15).

9.16.2   Maker of a database
The maker of a database is the person who takes the initiative in making it and who assumes the risks of investing in making it; subject to any agreement to the contrary (Reg.14)

9.16.3 Qualifications for database right
A database qualifies for the database right if –
(a) there has been a substantial investment in obtaining, verifying or presenting the contents of the database, irrespective of whether the database or any of its contents are works protected by copyright; (Reg.13);
(b) when it was made, the maker or one of the makers was –
  (i) an EEA national or a habitual resident within the EEA; or
  (ii) a body incorporated under the law of an EEA State, and which has its central administration or principal place of business within the EEA; or has its registered office within the EEA and its operations are linked on an ongoing basis with the economy of an EEA State; (Reg.18) or
  (iii) the Crown, or one or both of the Houses of Parliament. (Reg (14(3)(4))

9.16.4 Infringement of database right
(a) A person infringes database right if, without the consent of the owner of the right, he extracts or re-utilizes all, or a substantial part, of the contents of the database. (Reg. 16(1))
(b) "Extraction" means the permanent or temporary transfer of the contents of a database to another medium by any means or in any form; "re-utilization" means making the contents of a database available to the public by any means. (Reg.12(1))
(c) The repeated and systematic extraction or re-utilization of an insubstantial part of a database may amount to the extraction or re-utilization of a substantial part of the database. (Reg. 16(2))
(d) Making a copy of a database available for use on terms that it will, or may be returned, otherwise than for economic or commercial advantage, does not constitute extraction or re-utilization. (Reg.12 (2))
(e) The sale in the EEA of a copy of a database does not constitute extraction or re-utilization if the copy had previously been sold in the EEA by or with the consent of the owner of the database right. (Reg. 12(4))

9.16.5 Duration of database right
Database right expires 15 years after the end of the year in which the database was made, but if it is made available to the public before the end of that period the right expires 15 years after the end of the year in which it was made available. (Reg.17)

9.16.6   Exceptions to database right
         Database right is subject to the following exceptions.
         (a) A lawful user of a database which has been made available to the
             public may extract or re-utilize insubstantial parts for any purpose.
             (Reg.19(1))
         (b) Fair dealing with a substantial part of a database which has been
             made available to the public by a lawful user for purposes of
             illustration for teaching or research, unless for a commercial
             purpose, is not an infringement of the database right, provided the
             source is indicated. (Reg. 20(1))
         (c) Where a person has a right under an agreement to use a database
             which has been made available to the public, any term in the
             agreement purporting to prevent the user from extracting
             insubstantial parts of the contents, is void. (Reg. 19(2)).
         (d) Database right is not infringed by the extraction or re–utilisation of
             a substantial part of a database at a time when it was not possible by
             reasonable enquiry to identify the maker and it is reasonable to
             assume that the right has expired. (Reg. 21; see s.57 of the Act and
             para.13.2.15 below)
         (e) Database right is subject to exceptions corresponding to those which
             apply to works protected by copyright in the following cases –
                 (i)   use for Parliamentary or judicial proceedings;
                 (ii) Royal commissions and statutory enquiries;
                 (iii) as material open to public inspection or in official registers;
                 (iv) as material communicated to the Crown;
                 (v)   as material in public records;
                 (vi) use covered by statutory authority.
             (Sch.I of the Regulations; see ss.45, 47, 48, 49 and 50 of the Act, and
             para. 13.2.8 below)

9.16.7   Presumptions in legal proceedings in relation to databases
         For the purpose of legal proceedings it is presumed, unless the contrary
         is proved, that the name of the person purporting to be the maker of a
         database which appears on copies of it, is in fact the maker and that he
         met the prescribed conditions. (Reg.22)

9.16.8   Application of copyright provisions to database rights
         (a) The provisions of ss.90-93 (dealing with rights in copyright works),
             ss.96-98 (rights and remedies of copyright owner) and ss.101 and 102
             (rights and remedies of exclusive licensee) of the Act apply to
             database right and databases in which the right subsists as they apply
             to copyright and works in which copyright subsists. (Reg.23)

23

(b) Schedule 2 of the Regulations contain provisions which confer jurisdiction on the Copyright Tribunal over the licensing of database rights by licensing bodies. These provisions reproduce, mutatis mutandis, the corresponding provisions in Chapter VII of the 1988 Act; in particular the following sections:

ss.116,117–definitions of licensing body, licensing scheme, licence
s.118–reference to the Tribunal of a proposed licensing scheme
s.119–reference to the Tribunal of a licensing scheme
s.120–further reference of a scheme to the Tribunal
s.121–applications for a licence under a scheme
s.122–application for a review of Tribunal order made under s.121
s.123–effect of Tribunal order relating to a scheme
s.124–references and applications to Tribunal with regard to licences
s.125–reference to Tribunal of a proposed licence
s.126–reference to the Tribunal of an expiring licence
s.127–application for review of Tribunal order as to a licence
s.128–effect of Tribunal order relating to a licence
s.144–-powers exercisable in consequence of a report by the Monopolies and Mergers Commission

(paras. 1-15 of Schedule 2 of the Regulations; see also paras. 16.2-16.5, 17.1, 18.1, 19.1; 15.4 below).

9.16.9   (a) The Copyright and Rights in Databases Regulations 1997 do not affect any agreement made before 1 January 1998.

(b) No act done before 1 January 1998, or done after that date in pursuance of an agreement made before 1 January 1998, constitutes infringement of database right in a database.

9.17   Infringement - general principle

Subject to the exceptions to the rights of copyright owners summarized in paras. 12.1 - 18.2 below, the copyright in a protected work is infringed if anyone, without first obtaining the permission of the copyright owner, does, or authorizes another person to do, any of the acts listed above which are controlled by the copyright in the particular work; and the infringement takes place even if the infringing act does not affect the entire work, provided it affects a substantial part of it. (s.16(2)(3))

9.18   Whether or not a part is substantial does not depend solely upon quantity; a part may be substantial even if in length it is small in proportion to the whole work, but nevertheless by virtue of its content is an important part of the work.

9.19   Infringement by authorising
        Copyright is infringed not only by the person who actually carries out
        the infringing act, but by any person who authorizes another person to
        do the act.(s.16(2)) The meaning of "authorizes" has been considered
        by the courts in many cases; and different views have been expressed.
        In 1988 the House of Lords said that "authorise" means to grant, or
        purport to grant, expressly or by implication, the right to do the act
        complained of.

The Economic Rights of Copyright Owners - Secondary Rights

10.1   The copyright in a protected work is also infringed if anyone, without
        first obtaining the permission of the copyright owner, –
        (a) imports (otherwise than for his private and domestic use) an article
            which he knows or has reason to believe is an infringing copy of a
            work; (s.22)
        (b) possesses, trades in or distributes an article which he knows or has
            reason to believe is an infringing copy of the work; (s.23)
        (c) makes, imports, possesses or trades in an article specifically designed
            for making copies of the work knowing or having reason to believe
            that the article will be used for that purpose; (s.24(1))
        (d) transmits the work via a telecommunications system (other than a
            broadcasting or cable service) for example, a fax or telex message,
            knowing or having reason to believe that infringing copies of the
            work would be made through the reception of the transmission;
            (s.24(2))
        (e) gives permission for a place of public entertainment to be used for
            the performance of a literary, dramatic or musical work which
            amounts to an infringement, unless he had reasonable grounds for
            believing that the performance would not be an infringement; (s.25)
        (f) supplies apparatus which is used for infringing the copyright in a
            work by playing a sound recording, showing a film or receiving
            images or sounds by electronic means, if he knew or had reason to
            believe the apparatus would be so used or if he did not believe on
            reasonable grounds that it would not be so used; (s.26(1)(2))
        (g) supplies a copy of a sound recording or a film which is used to
            infringe copyright if when he supplied it he knew or had reason to
            believe that it, or a copy made from it, would be used for that
            purpose. (s.26(4))

10.2   Meaning of infringing copy
For the purpose of these secondary infringements, an infringing copy includes an article which, if it had been made in the United Kingdom by the person who made it outside the United Kingdom, would have constituted an infringement of the copyright in the work, or would have been a breach of an exclusive licence relating to the work. Such articles are often referred to as "parallel imports". (s.27(3)) This rule is subject to two qualifications –

(a) a general provision that section 27(3) does not apply to an article which may lawfully be imported into the United Kingdom by virtue of an enforceable European Community right; (s.27(5)) and

(b) a specific provision that a copy of a computer program which has been sold in any other EU State by or with the consent of the copyright owner is not an infringing copy for the purposes of section 27(3). (s.27(3A))

Special Anti-Piracy Provisions

11.1   Where copies of a copyright work are issued to the public in a form which incorporates an electronic system designed to prevent copying of the work, any person who makes or trades in or advertises a device specifically designed to circumvent that copying protection, or who publishes information intended to help persons to circumvent the copy protection, commits an infringement of the copyright in the work. (s.296)

11.2   Where programmes containing copyright material are broadcast in an encoded form intended only for reception by persons who have legitimately acquired decoding or metering equipment, any person who dishonestly receives such a programme with the intention of avoiding payment for the right to do so, commits an offence. Moreover, those who make such programmes, or transmit them, have the same right of action as a copyright owner has in respect of infringement, against anyone who makes, imports or trades in equipment designed to enable individuals to receive such programmes illicitly or who publishes information to enable individuals to do so. (ss.297, 298)

Exceptions to Copyright Owner's Exclusive Rights

12.1   Exceptions to copyright are of two kinds. First, there are specific kinds of use where Parliament has decided that it is in the public interest that the work should be used without the need to obtain the copyright owner's permission (though in some cases he may be entitled to some remuneration). Secondly, the Act empowers the Secretary of State in certain cases and the Copyright Tribunal in other cases to override the exercise by the copyright owner of his rights, either by granting a licence when the copyright owner has decided not to do so, or, in cases where the copyright owner is prepared to grant a licence on certain conditions, by varying those conditions.

12.2 The provisions dealing with the first category of specific exceptions are contained in some 54 sections (ss.29-75); and the powers of the Secretary of State and the Copyright Tribunal are contained in another 36 sections. In this brief Guide, it is impossible to cover, even in the most condensed form, all these provisions. What follows is simply a summary of the salient provisions indicating the kinds of use which may be covered by an exception; and the principal situations where the powers of the Secretary of State and the Copyright Tribunal may be invoked. Anyone, whether a copyright owner or user, who thinks that he may be affected by an exception must refer to the specific terms of the Act and it would be wise for him, in all cases, to obtain professional advice.

Specific Exceptions

13.1 It is important to note that all the following exceptions do not apply to all categories of works; for example, fair dealing for purposes of criticism or review applies to all categories of works; whereas the inclusion of short passages in a collection for educational use only applies to published literary and dramatic works.

13.2 Use of a work in any of the following ways, or for any of the following purposes, does not infringe the copyright in the work –

13.2.1 Fair dealing for research or private study with a literary, dramatic, musical or artistic work or typographical arrangement; provided that, in the case of a database, the source is indicated. (s.29; see also para. 9.16.6(b) above)

13.2.2 Fair dealing for criticism or review of a work or of a performance of a work, provided the identity of the author and the title of the work are acknowledged. (s.30(1))

13.2.3 Fair dealing with any work other than a photograph for reporting current events, provided the identity of the author is acknowledged. (s.30(2))

13.2.4   Fair dealing is an elusive concept; it has never been defined by statute, nor is there any comprehensive definitive judicial interpretation. Broadly speaking, it covers what an average user of a work might be expected to do with it for his personal use e.g. an individual copying an extract from a literary work for future reference, even if he uses a photocopier to make the copy; but not, of course, making a copy for another person. Under the principal international copyright convention - the Berne Convention - dealing with a work would not be regarded as fair if it conflicts with the normal commercial exploitation of the work or if it unreasonably prejudices the legitimate interests of the copyright owner. It would not be fair to an author who earns his livelihood by writing school text books for copies of his books to be made, without his permission, in order to supply a class of students for their "private study". And, of course, copying done in consideration of a payment or for commercial purposes would not be fair dealing. The Act expressly provides that in relation to a database research for a commercial purpose is not fair dealing. (s.29(5)

13.2.5   Incidental inclusion of any work in an artistic work, sound recording, film, broadcast, or cable programme; for example, a shot in a documentary about life in London showing a contemporary painting hanging on the wall of an apartment. (s.31(1))

13.2.6   Educational use in any of the following ways –
(a) Copying any description of work, other than a typographical arrangement, for the purpose of instruction or preparing for instruction, by either the person giving or the person receiving instruction provided the copying is not done by means of equipment for making facsimile or multiple copies or for copying by electronic means. (s.32(1)(2))
(b) Copying for the purposes of examinations. (s.32(3)(4))
(c) Including a short passage from a published literary or dramatic work in a collection intended for educational use and which consists mainly of non copyright material. (s.33)
(d) Performing a literary, dramatic or musical work before an audience of teachers and pupils at a teaching establishment. (s.34(1))
(e) Playing or showing a sound recording, film, broadcast or cable programme before such an audience for the purposes of instruction. (s.34(2))

(f) Recording a broadcast or cable programme or a copy of such a recording, by an educational establishment for educational purposes; this covers, of course, the right to record a work of any description included in the broadcast or cable programme; but it is important to note that this exception does not apply if there is a licensing scheme, certified by the Secretary of State, under which licences are available for authorising such recordings. (s.35(1)(2))

(g) Copying passages from published literary, dramatic or musical works, or typographical arrangements, by an educational establishment for instruction purposes provided that no more than 1% of a work is copied under this exception in any one calendar quarter. It is to be noted that this exception does not apply if licences authorising the copying are available. (s.36)

(h) Lending copies of a work by an educational establishment. (s.36A)

13.2.7   **Use by libraries and archives**

Both the 1988 Act itself and the Copyright (Librarians and Archivists) (Copying of Copyright Material) Regulations 1989 (1989 SI No.1212) contain a number of rules which govern the application of these exceptions. The following sub–paragraphs do not purport to summarise all the rules; they merely indicate the more important ones; reference should be made to the relevant provisions in the Act (ss.38-43) and the Regulations.

(a) The librarian of a prescribed library may make and supply to a member of the public –

    (i) one copy of one article in an issue of a periodical;

    (ii) one copy of a part of a published literary, dramatic or musical work. (ss.38, 39)

The Act requires regulations made by the Secretary of State to include the following conditions on the exercise of this authority to make copies –

    (i) the librarian must be satisfied that the person seeking a copy requires it for research or private study, and will not use it for any other purpose;

    (ii) a copy supplied of part of a work must not exceed more than a reasonable proportion of the work;

    (iii) the person receiving the copy must pay for the cost of producing it.

(b) The librarian of a prescribed library may make and supply to another prescribed library a copy of an article in a periodical or a copy of the whole (or part) of a published literary, dramatic or musical work. (s.41)

(c) The librarian or archivist of a prescribed library or archive may make a copy of any literary, dramatic or musical work (including any illustrations), or of a typographical arrangement, for the purpose of preserving or replacing the work in its permanent collection. (s.42(1))

This authority may only be exercised if it is not reasonably practicable to buy a copy for this purpose. (s.42(2))

(d) The librarian or archivist of a prescribed library or archive may make and supply to a member of the public, who requires it for purposes of research or private study, a copy of an unpublished literary, dramatic or musical work (including illustrations) provided the copyright owner has not prohibited the copying of the work. (s.43(1)(2))

Regulations made by the Secretary of State must include the following conditions for the exercise of this authority –

(i)   the librarian or archivist must be satisfied that the person seeking the copy requires it for research or private study, and will not use it for any other purpose;

(ii) no one may be furnished with more than one copy of the same material;

(iii) the person receiving the copy must pay for the cost of producing it. (s.43(3))

(e) The copyright in any work is not infringed by the lending by a public library of a book within the public lending right scheme established by the Public Lending Right Act 1979. (s.40A(1))

(f) The copyright in any work is not infringed by the lending of copies of it by a prescribed library or archive (other than a public library) which is not conducted for profit. (s.40A(2))

Prescribed libraries and archives are those which are designated by regulations.

13.2.8   Public administration

Copyright is not infringed by anything done in relation to any description of work for the purposes of –

(a) Parliamentary or judicial proceedings, including the reporting of such proceedings. (s.45)

(b) The proceedings of a Royal Commission or statutory enquiry, including the reporting of such proceedings when held in public. (s.46)

(c) Copying material open to public inspection under a statutory requirement, or which is in a statutory register, in order to –
  (i)   make information contained in the material available to the public,
  (ii) enable more convenient inspection of it, or
  (iii) issue copies of the material to the public when it contains matters of general scientific, technical, commercial or economic interest. (s.47)
(d) Making, by the Crown, a copy of a literary, dramatic, musical or artistic work which has been communicated to the Crown by the copyright owner, provided the copy is made for a purpose contemplated by the copyright owner when the work was communicated; this includes issuing copies of the work to the public provided, in this case, that it has been previously published. (s.48)
(e) Making, and supplying to any person, a copy of any material comprised in public records open to public inspection. (s.49)
(f) Doing an act specifically authorised by an Act of Parliament. (s.50)

13.2.9   Computer programs
It is not an infringement of the copyright in a computer program for a lawful user of a copy of the program–
(a) to make a back up copy which is necessary for the purposes of the lawful use; (s.50A)
(b) in the case of a program expressed in low level language, to convert it into a higher level language and, in the course of the conversion, to copy it (i.e. decompile it), provided–
  (i) the decompiling is necessary in order to obtain the information needed to create an independent program which can be operated with the decompiled, or another, program; and
  (ii) the information so obtained is not used for any other purpose; (s.50B)
(c) to copy or adapt it, provided –
  (i) the copying or adapting is necessary for its lawful use; and
  (ii) is not prohibited by any agreement regulating the circumstances in which the use of the program is lawful. (s.50C)
It is important to note that in the case of the forms of use permitted by sections 50A and 50B any contractual term purporting to prohibit such use is expressly declared to be void. (s.296A)

31

13.2.10 Databases
A person who has a right to use a database (whether under a licence from the owner of the copyright in the database or otherwise) does not commit an infringement of that copyright by doing anything which is necessary in order that he may have access to or use the contents of the database. (s.50D) Any contractual term purporting to prohibit a use of a database permitted by s.50D is void. (s.296B).

13.2.11 Designs
Making an article to a design which is embodied in a design document (such as a drawing) or in a model, or copying such an article, unless that article is itself an artistic work or a typeface. (s.51)

13.2.12 Artistic works
(a) Where an artistic work has been commercially exploited, with the copyright owner's permission, by the marketing of copies, then 25 years after the end of the year of first marketing the copyright in the work is not infringed by anything done in relation to those copies or by making more copies. (s.52(1)(2))
(b) Where an artistic work consists of the design of a typeface and articles specifically designed for producing material in that typeface have been marketed with the permission of the copyright owner, then 25 years after the year of first marketing the copyright in the work is not infringed by doing anything in relation to those articles or making more articles. (s.55)

13.2.13 Typefaces
The normal use of a typeface for the purpose of typing, composing text, type setting or printing, or possessing any article for such a purpose or doing anything in relation to material produced in such use. (s.54)

13.2.14 Electronic works
Making a copy of a copy of a work in electronic form by a person who has purchased the copy, provided a copy could have been lawfully made by the vendor, either by virtue of contract or by an express or implied rule of law. When a copyright owner sells a copy he may, therefore, stipulate conditions which will govern not only what the purchaser may do, but which also bind any person to whom the purchaser transfers the copy. (s.56)

13.2.15 Anonymous and pseudonymous works
Any act done in relation to a literary, dramatic, musical or artistic work when it is not possible to ascertain the identity of the author and it is reasonable to assume that copyright has expired or that the author had died more than 70 years previously; but this exception does not apply to works in which Crown copyright, or the copyright of an international organisation, subsists. (s.57)

13.2.16 Use of the notes of spoken words
The use of a record, in writing or otherwise, of spoken words for the purpose of reporting current events, broadcasting or inclusion in a cable programme service does not infringe the copyright in the words as a literary work provided the speaker did not prohibit the making of the record and its use was authorised by the person who was lawfully in possession of it. (s.58)

13.2.17 Public reading or recitation
The public reading or recitation by one person of a reasonable extract from a published literary or dramatic work, or the making of a sound recording or the broadcasting or inclusion in a cable programme service of such a reading or recitation. (s.59)

13.2.18 Abstracts
Copying or issuing copies to the public, of an abstract of an article on a scientific or technical subject published in a periodical containing both the abstract and the article; but this exception does not apply if there is a licensing scheme, certified by the Secretary of State, which provides for the granting of licences for the making of such copies. (s.60)

13.2.19 Recordings for folk song archive
Making a sound recording of a folk song in order to include it in a designated archive, and supplying copies of the recording from the archive, in accordance with prescribed conditions, provided –
(i) the words are unpublished and of unknown authorship,
(ii) making the recording does not infringe any other copyright, and
(iii) making the recording is not prohibited by a performer. (s.61)

13.2.20 Buildings and artistic works on public display
Making a graphic representation, a photograph or a film of a building or of sculptures or models or works of artistic craftsmanship which are permanently situated in public. (s.62)

13.2.21 Advertisement for the sale of artistic works
Copying, or issuing copies to the public, of an artistic work for the purpose of advertising its sale. (s.63)

13.2.22 Copying an earlier work by its artist
Making a copy by an artist of an earlier work of his for the purpose of a later work provided he does not reproduce the main design of the first work. (s.64)

13.2.23 Reconstruction of buildings
Anything done in relation to a building or drawings or plans relating to the building, for the purpose of reconstructing it. (s.65)

13.2.24 Sound recording played for charitable purposes
Playing a sound recording as part of the activities of an institution whether it be a club, society or other organisation, whose main objects are charitable. (s.67)

13.2.25 Broadcasters' ephemeral recording right
Making a recording of any description of work, other than a typographical arrangement, by a person who has been authorised to broadcast the work or to include it in a cable programme, if the recording is made solely for the purposes of the broadcast or cable programme and is destroyed within 28 days after being first used for that purpose. (s.68)

13.2.26 Recordings for supervision of broadcasts and cable programmes
Making or using recordings of any description of work by the BBC, the Independent Television Commission, the Radio Authority or the Broadcasting Standards Commission for the purpose of carrying out their duties under the Broadcasting Acts 1990 and 1996. (s.69)

13.2.27 Recordings for time shifting
Recording, for private and domestic use, a broadcast or cable programme, including any work contained in it, so that it may be viewed or listened to at a more convenient time. (s.70)

13.2.28 Photographs of broadcasts and cable programmes
Taking a photograph, for private and domestic use, of an image in a television broadcast or cable programme, does not infringe the copyright in the broadcast, cable programme or any film contained in it. (s.71)

13.2.29 Free showings of broadcasts and cable programmes
Showing or playing in public a broadcast or cable programme, and any sound recording or film included in it, if the audience has not paid for admission to the showing. (s.72)

13.2.30 Re-transmission of broadcasts in cable programmes
Where a broadcast, made from a place in the United Kingdom, is by reception and immediate re-transmission, included in a cable programme service –
(a) The copyright in the broadcast is not infringed –
    (i) if the inclusion is required under section 79A or paragraph 4 of Part III of Schedule 12 of the Broadcasting Act 1990; or
    (ii) if, and to the extent that, the broadcast is made for reception in the area in which the cable service is provided and is part of a qualifying service. (s.73(2))
Subsection (6) of section 73 of the 1988 Act contains a list of qualifying services; but under subsection (8) the Secretary of State may add new services to, or remove services from, the list. In invoking the exceptions in this section it is important to ensure that the current list is used. The services in the list in force on 31 December 1997 are set out in Appendix 4 to this Guide.
(b) The copyright in any work included in the broadcast is not infringed if the broadcast is made for reception in the area in which the cable service is provided; but if the making of the broadcast was an infringement of the copyright in the work, the re-transmission of the work by the cable service shall be taken into account in assessing the damages for that infringement. (s.73(3))
(c) Where the broadcast is included in the cable service pursuant to a requirement under the Broadcasting Act and the area in which the cable service is provided falls outside, to some extent, the area of reception in which the broadcast is made, the inclusion in the cable service of a work contained in the broadcast shall, in respect of the extended cable service area, be treated as licensed by the owner of the copyright in the work subject to the payment to him by the broadcaster of reasonable remuneration, which in the absence of agreement shall be fixed by the Copyright Tribunal. (s.73(4))

13.2.31 Broadcasting and inclusion in cable programmes of sound recordings
(a) Where –
    (i) there is a licensing body with a mandate to grant licences for the broadcasting or inclusion in cable programmes of sound recordings, or could procure the grant of such a licence; and

(ii) the licensing body has refused to grant, or procure the grant, to a broadcaster or operator of a cable service, of such a licence on terms as to payment and needletime which are acceptable to the broadcaster or cable operator, or

(iii) in the case where the broadcaster or cable operator already has a licence, and the licence includes terms limiting needletime, and the licensing body has refused to remove or modify those terms, or procure their removal or modification, to the satisfaction of the broadcaster or cable operator,

the broadcaster, or cable operator, may, subject to the conditions and procedures outlined below, proceed to broadcast sound recordings or include them in his cable service as if he was the holder of a licence granted by the owners of the copyright in the recordings. (ss.135A, 135C(1))

(b) The salient conditions and procedures which must be complied with and followed may be summarized as follows –

(i) before proceeding to broadcast recordings or include them in his cable service pursuant to sub-paragraph (a), the broadcaster or cable operator must give notice of his intention to do so to the licensing body asking the latter to propose terms;

(ii) after receiving the licensing body's proposals, or after a reasonable time if he receives no terms, the broadcaster or cable operator must notify the licensing body of the date when he intends to broadcast or include the recordings in his service, and of the payment he intends to make;

(iii) the broadcaster or cable operator must give reasonable notice to the Copyright Tribunal of his intention to broadcast or include works in his service, and the date when he intends to start; and must apply to the Tribunal to settle the terms of the licence;

(iv) the Tribunal must hear and determine the application, making such order as it considers reasonable after taking into account, inter alia, certain factors specified in the Act; and may, subject to conditions, review and modify such order;

(v) until the Tribunal has made an order the broadcaster or cable operator must make payments to the licensing body, which must be made at not less than quarterly intervals in arrears, of the amounts set out in the licensing body's proposals, or if the broadcaster or cable operator considers those proposals to be unreasonable, of the amounts he had notified to the licensing body that he intended to pay;

(vi) all payments made under (v) must be adjusted subsequently to conform to the Tribunal's order when made.
(ss.135B, 135C, 135D, 135E, 135F and 135G)

13.2.32   Administration of cable re–transmission right
(a) The right of the owner of the copyright in a literary, dramatic, musical or artistic work, sound recording or film to authorise or prohibit the inclusion in a cable programme service of a broadcast containing that work, recording or film, when the broadcast was transmitted from another EEA member State, may only be exercised through a licensing body. (s.144A(1)(2))
(b) Where a copyright owner has not transferred management of his cable re–transmission right to a licensing body, the body administering rights of that category is deemed to be mandated to manage the copyright owner's rights. (s.144A(3))
(c) In the situation described in (b) the copyright owner has the same rights and obligations resulting from licensing agreements with cable operators as have the copyright owners who have transferred their rights to the licensing body. The copyright owner must claim such rights within three years from the date of the cable re-transmission to which the rights relate. (s.144A(4)(5))

13.2.33   Copies of broadcasts, cable programmes for handicapped persons
Copies of broadcasts or cable programmes and of any works included in them made for the use of handicapped persons by a body designated by the Secretary of State. (s.74)

13.2.34   Recordings for archives
Recordings of a broadcast or cable programme or any work included in it made for archival purposes by a body designated by the Secretary of State. (s.75)

Extended and revived copyright - savings protecting third party interests

14.   The Duration of Copyright and Rights in Performances Regulations 1995 contain the following special rules to protect the interests of third parties.

14.1   In respect of every work in which revived copyright subsists a statutory licence is available to anyone in respect of any act covered by the revived copyright subject only to the payment of reasonable

remuneration which, in the absence of agreement, is determined by the Copyright Tribunal. This licence is not available –
(a) unless the intending user gives reasonable notice to the owner of the revived right;
(b) if a licence to do the act contemplated is available from a licensing body.
(Reg.24)

14.2   In respect of a work in which revived copyright subsists it is not an infringement after 1 January 1996 –
(i) to do anything in relation to the work, pursuant to arrangements for exploiting it made before 1 January 1995 at a time when copyright did not subsist in the work;
(ii) to issue to the public copies made before 1 July 1995 at a time when copyright did not subsist in the work;
(iii) to do anything in relation to a literary, dramatic, musical or artistic work or a film –
    (a) which was made before 1 January 1996, or
    (b) which was made pursuant to arrangements made before 1 January 1996, and which contains a copy of the work in which revived copyright subsists or is an adaptation of that work, if the copy or adaptation was made before 1 July 1995 at a time when copyright did not subsist in the work, or the copy or adaptation was made pursuant to arrangements made before 1 July 1995 at a time when copyright did not subsist in the work;
(iv) to do any act in relation to the work if the act is done at a time, or pursuant to arrangements made at a time, when the name and address of a person entitled to authorise the act could not by reasonable enquiry be ascertained.
(Reg.23)

Powers of Secretary of State and Copyright Tribunal

15.   The Secretary of State may –

15.1   (a) Impose a compulsory licence authorising members of the public to rent copies of literary, dramatic, musical or artistic works, sound recordings or films subject to the payment of reasonable remuneration. (s.66)

It is to be noted that –

(i) the remuneration is to be the subject of negotiation, and in default of agreement, to be determined by the Copyright Tribunal;

(ii) this power may not be invoked if there is in operation a voluntary licensing scheme certified by the Secretary of State under which rental licences may be obtained.

15.2   (b) Extend the compulsory licensing provisions of sections 135A - 135G (which deal with sound recordings) to any other category of works. (s.135H)

15.3   (c) Extend licensing schemes and licences granted by copyright owners covering the making of reprographic copies of published literary, dramatic, musical or artistic works and typographical arrangements by educational establishments for instruction purposes to similar works and arrangements not otherwise covered by those schemes or licences. (ss.137, 138)

15.3   (d) (i) Institute an enquiry as to whether provision is required to authorise the copying of published literary, dramatic, musical or artistic works or typographical arrangements by educational establishments for instruction purposes, because such copying is not covered by existing licences or schemes; (s.140) and

(ii) if the person holding the enquiry makes a recommendation that such a scheme is needed, and within one year from that recommendation no voluntary scheme has been established, the Secretary of State may impose a free compulsory licence in accordance with the recommendation. (s.141)

15.4   (e) Modify the conditions in a licence granted by a copyright owner, or direct the grant of a licence in a case where the copyright owner has refused one, if the Monopolies and Mergers Commission has reported that those conditions, or the refusal to grant the licence, operate against the public interest; provided, however, that this power may not be exercised if to do so would contravene any convention relating to copyright to which the United Kingdom is a party. (s.144)

Copyright Tribunal - Jurisdiction - General

16.1   Broadly speaking, the Copyright Tribunal has jurisdiction where rights are either licensed pursuant to a "licensing scheme" or are licensed by a "licensing body" (either under a licensing scheme or otherwise). It does not have jurisdiction when rights in a specfic work are individually licensed by an individual copyright owner; provided, however, that the copyright owner does not fall within the extended meaning given to "licensing body".

16.2 The meanings of the two terms "licensing scheme" and "licensing body" are therefore central to an understanding of the functions of the Tribunal and the limits of its jurisdiction.

16.3 A "licensing scheme" is not itself a licence; it is simply a statement promulgated by a person who is in a position to issue licences, which specifies the cases in which the operator of the scheme is prepared to grant licences, and the terms which would be included in those licences. (s.116(1))

16.4 A "licensing body" is defined by the Act as –
"a society or other organisation which has as its main object, or one of its main objects, the negotiation or granting, either as owner or prospective owner of copyright or as agent for him, of copyright licences, and whose objects include the granting of licences covering works of more than one author". (s.116(2))

16.5 It should be noted that –
(a) A licensing scheme may be operated by a person who is not a licensing body. Thus, a popular playwright who chooses to administer his own rights of copyright may publish the terms on which he is prepared to license performances of his plays in various situations, one set of terms applying to performances in village halls, another to performances for charitable purposes, another to performances in theatres in the provinces and a fourth set of terms applicable to West End theatre productions.
(b) A person or enterprise may be a licensing body even if not engaged in collective administration as normally understood. Thus, an individual music publisher who administers reproduction rights on behalf of more than one composer and is prepared to grant licences covering all such rights within his catalogue would be a licensing body; as would be a book publisher who is prepared to grant photocopying licences covering two or more of his authors.

The Tribunal's Jurisdiction Over Licensing Schemes

17.1   The kinds of disputes over licensing schemes which may be referred to the Tribunal are –
(a) disputes over the terms of a scheme which a licensing body proposes to operate; (s.118)
(b) disputes over the terms of a scheme which is already in operation, irrespective of whether or not the operator of the scheme is a licensing body; (s.119)
(c) disputes over a revision of an order of the Tribunal made under either (a) or (b); (s.120)
(d) disputes over the refusal of the operator of a scheme (who may or may not be a licensing body) to grant a licence to an applicant claiming to be covered by the scheme; (s.121)
(e) a dispute over the revision of an order made under (d). (s.122)

17.2   Not all licensing schemes are within the Tribunal's jurisdiction; the schemes in respect of which disputes may be referred to the Tribunal are those which relate to licences for –
(a) Copying works
(b) Rental or lending of copies of works to the public
(c) Performing, showing or playing works in public
(d) Broadcasting works or including them in cable programme services. (s.117)

The Tribunal's Jurisdiction Over Licences From Licensing Bodies

18.1   This jurisdiction is limited to disputes about individual licences sought from, or offered by, a licensing body where there is no applicable licensing scheme; the Tribunal has no jurisdiction if a licence is to be granted by a copyright owner who is not a licensing body.

18.2   This jurisdiction, therefore, exists where there is a user of copyright material who does not fall into a particular class covered by a licensing scheme e.g. the BBC, and who requires a licence from a licensing body e.g. the Performing Right Society (which administers the broadcasting rights in copyright music). Under this jurisdiction, a dispute between such a user and a licensing body regarding the refusal of the licensing body to issue a licence, or the terms of the licence offered, or regarding the revision of an order of the Tribunal fixing the terms of a licence, could be referred to the Tribunal. (ss.124-128)

41

18.3   As in the case of licensing schemes the Tribunal's jurisdiction is limited to licences from licensing bodies relating to –
(a) Copying works
(b) Rental or lending of copies of works
(c) Performing, showing or playing works in public
(d) Broadcasting works or including them in cable programme services. (s.124)

The Tribunal's Powers

19.1   In a dispute referred to the Tribunal it may, by order –
(a) confirm a licensing scheme, or vary its terms;
   (ss.118(3), 119(3),120(4))
(b) confirm the terms of a licence, or vary them; (s.125(3))
(c) confirm the refusal of a licensing body to issue a licence, or make an order authorising the applicant to act as if he had a licence, on condition that he complies with the terms fixed by the Tribunal. (ss.121(4), 122(3), 126(4))

19.2   In exercising its powers, the Tribunal is required to take account of certain factors, which vary depending on the nature of the dispute. These factors are specified –
(a) in the case of licensing schemes and licences generally, in s.129;
(b) in the case of licences for reprographic copying, in s.130;
(c) in the case of licences for educational copying of broadcast material, in s.131;
(d) in the case of licences in respect of sound recordings, films, broadcasts or cable programmes containing entertainment or other events, in s.132;
(e) in the case of the determination of the amount payable for a licence covering the rental of sound recordings, films or computer programs, in s.133;
(f) in the case of licences in respect of works included in re–transmissions, in s.134.

Moral Rights

20.1   In addition to the author's economic rights described in the preceding paragraphs, the 1988 Act makes provision for moral rights. These are the two rights required by the Berne Copyright Convention to be provided by the national legislation of all member countries. They

consist of the right of an author, when a work of his is presented to the public –
(a) to be identified as its author, and
(b) to be able to prevent any distortion of the work which would prejudice his reputation as an author.

The first right is known as the right of paternity, and the second, the right of integrity.

20.2   The provisions for these rights are contained in Chapter IV of the Act in a somewhat complex code in ss.77-89, 94, 95. The copyright statutes of the United Kingdom have not previously provided for these rights, so there is no established practice or body of case law to assist in the interpretation of these new statutory provisions. What follows is a summary of the salient features of Chapter IV.

20.3.   The persons entitled to moral rights are –
(a) the authors of copyright literary, dramatic, musical or artistic works; and
(b) the directors of copyright films. (ss.77(1), 80(1))

20.4   Provided copyright under the Act subsists in the work or the film, its author, or director, as the case may be, is entitled to moral rights, irrespective of his nationality or place of residence.

20.5   The Act specifies the circumstances in which each right may be claimed, depending upon the type of work; but broadly speaking, each right becomes exercisable whenever the work, or film, is published commercially, or is otherwise presented or released to the public. (ss.77(2)-(7), 80(2)-(7)) Each right is subject to its own set of rules which are summarized as follows.

20.6   The paternity right
(a) Unless the author or director specifies a particular form of identification any reasonable form may be used. (s.77(8))
(b) The right does not arise in the following cases –
    (i)   in relation to computer programs, typeface designs or computer-generated works; (s.79(2))
    (ii) where the initial ownership of the copyright has vested in someone other than the author or director e.g. where it vests in the author's or director's employer; (s.79(3))
    (iii) in relation to an act which does not amount to an infringement of copyright by virtue of certain specified exceptions; (s.79(4))

(iv) in relation to a work made for the purpose of reporting current events; (s.79(5))

(v) in relation to publication in a newspaper, magazine or similar periodical or an encyclopedia, dictionary, year book or other collective work of reference when the work was either made, or was made available, for the purposes of such publication; (s.79(6))

(vi) in relation to works in which Crown or Parliamentary copyright subsists. (s.79(7))

(c) The right may not be enforced unless it has been asserted, which may be general or specific i.e. in relation only to a specified form of use. (s.78(1))

(d) Assertion may be effected by an appropriate statement in an instrument assigning the copyright in the work, or by any instrument in writing signed by the author or director. In the case of an artistic work, it may also be asserted by the identification of the author on the original work or on a copy of it or on the frame or mount to which it is attached. (s.78(2)(3))

(e) Broadly speaking, an assertion, depending on the way in which it is made, binds anyone to whose notice it has been expressly brought or who it would be reasonable to assume would be aware of it. (s.78(4))

20.7   The integrity right

(a) This right does not have to be asserted.

(b) This right does not arise in the following cases –

(i)   in relation to computer programs or computer-generated works; (s.81(2))

(ii) works made for the purpose of reporting current events; (s.81(3))

(iii) in relation to works published in a newspaper or a magazine or similar periodical, or in an encyclopedia, dictionary, year book or other collective work of reference if the work was made, or made available, for such publication; (s.81(4))

(iv) in relation to pseudonymous and anonymous works where it may be assumed that copyright has expired due to the death of the author; (s.81(5))

(v) in relation to any act done for the purpose of –
    (aa) avoiding the commission of an offence;
    (bb) complying with a statutory duty;
    (cc) the avoidance by the BBC of the broadcasting of anything which might offend good taste or decency, or which might be likely to encourage or incite crime, disorder or to be offensive to public feeling. (s.81(6))

(vi) Where the copyright in a work originally vested in someone other than the author (e.g. his employer) or the work is one in which Crown or Parliamentary copyright subsists, and the author of the work has not been identified, his integrity right is not infringed by anything done with the authority of the copyright owner. This applies also to the director of a film. The reason for this exclusion is presumably the Government view that if an author or director has not been identified, then neither can be injuriously affected by mutilation or distortion of his work or film. But the exclusion goes further: even if the author or director is identified, no act of mutilation or distortion will be regarded as an infringement of the integrity right if there is a clear and prominent indication that the author (or director) had not consented to that act. (ss.82, 178 – "sufficient disclaimer")

21.   The two moral rights and the special privacy right (see para. 25 below) last for the full period of the copyright in the work in question. (s.86)

22.   The person entitled to either the moral rights or the special privacy right (see para. 25 below) may consent to the doing of any act which would otherwise infringe those rights. There is no requirement that the consent must be in writing. (s.87(1))

23.   Both the moral rights and the privacy right (see para. 25 below) may be waived; but the instrument of waiver must be in writing. The rights may not be assigned. (ss.87(2)(3), 94)

24.   On the death of an author, film director or person entitled to a privacy right, (see para. 25 below) the moral rights and the privacy right pass to –
(a) the person designated in the will;
(b) in default of designation, the person to whom copyright in the work passes under the will;
(c) in default of (a) or (b), to the legal personal representatives. (s.95)

45

25.1   The privacy right
Chapter IV also contains a special provision, strictly speaking unrelated to moral rights, protecting the privacy of a person who commissions a photograph or film for private or domestic purposes, eg. wedding photographs.

25.2   Where copyright subsists in such a photograph or film, the person who commissioned it has a right not to have –
(a) copies issued to the public;
(b) the work exhibited in public;
(c) the work broadcast or included in a cable programme. (s.85)

25.3   The privacy right may not be exercised in relation to an act which does not, by virtue of the following provisions, constitute an infringement of copyright –
s.31 (incidental inclusion) see para. 13.2.5 above
s.45(parliamentary and judicial proceedings) see para. 13.2.8(a) above
s.46 (Royal Commissions and statutory enquiries) see para. 13.2.8(b) above
s.50 (acts specifically authorised by statute) see para. 13.2.8(f) above
ss.57 or 66A (assumption of expiry of copyright) see para. 13.2.15 above

26.   False attribution of authorship
Chapter IV also protects a person against the false attribution to him of the authorship of a literary, dramatic, musical or artistic work, or of having been the director of a film. This right lasts until 20 years after a person's death. (ss.84, 86(2))

The Enforcement of Copyright

27.   Although copyright is a property right, it is intangible and cannot be protected by physical means like other forms of property. If it is not respected it can only be enforced by legal proceedings; these may be civil or criminal.
An infringement of the moral rights, the privacy right or the right not to have authorship falsely attributed is actionable as a breach of a statutory duty. (s.103)

28.1   Infringement actions
Civil proceedings, i.e. an infringement action, may be brought by –
(a) the copyright owner, or
(b) subject to certain rules, an exclusive licensee. (ss.96, 101)

28.2   The copyright owner, or the licensee, does not have to be entitled to the entire copyright in the work; if the right alleged to have been infringed is the right to broadcast a work, all the plaintiff need establish is that he is the owner, or exclusive licensee, of the broadcasting right; and it does not matter that he does not own or control the right to make copies or any other right in the work.

28.3   In an infringement action the remedies available to the copyright owner, if successful, are –
(a) an injunction prohibiting the infringer from committing further infringing acts;
(b) damages in respect of economic loss suffered as a result of the infringement or an account of the profits made by the infringer;
(c) delivery to him of infringing copies and articles designed for making infringing copies;
(d) special additional damages where the infringement was particularly flagrant or the benefit enjoyed by the infringer was excessive, and
(e) the payment of his costs. (ss.96(2), 97)

28.4   Powers of seizure
In addition, a copyright owner may, without instituting an infringement action, obtain an order from the High Court for delivery of infringing copies of his work in the possession of a third party and, if such an order has been made, he may, subject to certain safeguards, himself take possession of infringing copies of his work which are publicly displayed for sale or hire. (ss.99,100)

28.5   Evidence
In an infringement action it is necessary, naturally, for the plaintiff to establish that the work in question is protected by copyright and that he is the owner, or exclusive licensee, of the copyright or of the relevant component right. Strict proof of these matters requires evidence as to –
(a) the nationality or citizenship of the author;
(b) whether he is alive or dead, and, if the latter, when he died;
(c) alternatively, the place and date of first publication;
(d) the year in which the work was made or, in the case of a film or sound recording the year in which it was first released;
(e) in the case of a cable programme, the year in which it was included in a cable service;
(f) the documents establishing his claim to be owner or licensee.

28.6   **Presumptions**

In many infringement actions none of these matters are seriously in dispute, whereas – particularly in the case of foreign works – it may be extremely difficult and costly to bring witnesses or produce original documents to establish these matters. In order, therefore, that copyright owners are not unreasonably prevented from enforcing their rights, the law stipulates that courts may make certain presumptions as to certain facts. Under the 1988 Act the principal presumptions are –

28.6.1   Actions involving literary, dramatic, musical or artistic works

(i)   A person whose name appears on a work is presumed, until the contrary is proved, to be the author; (s.104(1)(2))

(ii) where the author's name does not appear on the work but that of the publisher does, then unless the contrary is proved, the publisher is presumed to be the owner of the copyright; (s.104(1)(4))

(iii) if the author of a work is dead or his identity cannot be easily ascertained, in the absence of evidence to the contrary, the work is presumed to be original and the plaintiff's statements as to the first publication of the work are presumed to be correct. (s.104(5))

28.6.2   Actions involving sound recordings

Information on the label as to –

(i) the owner of the copyright, and

(ii) the date and place of first publication,

is presumed to be correct until the contrary is proved. (s.105(1))

28.6.3   Actions involving films

Information as to the following matters, on copies of the film issued to the public or in statements carried on films shown to the public, broadcast or included in cable programmes, is presumed to be correct until the contrary is proved –

(i) the name of the director or producer,

(ii) the name of the principal director, the author of the screenplay, the author of the dialogue or the composer of music specifically created for and used in the film,

(iii) the name of the owner of the copyright, and

(iv) in the case of copies issued to the public, the date and place of first publication. (s.105(2)(5))

28.6.4   Actions involving computer programs

Information on copies of the program issued to the public in electronic form as to –

(i) the owner of the copyright, and

(ii) the date of first publication or of the first issue to the public of copies in electronic form,

is presumed to be correct until the contrary is proved. (s.105(3))

28.6.5   Withdrawal of privilege against self-incrimination
In civil proceedings relating to the infringement of intellectual property rights a party may not refuse to answer questions the answers to which might incriminate him. Refusal to answer amounts to contempt of court. Any statement or admission made by a party in compliance with this rule may not be used in evidence against him in criminal proceedings. (s.72 Supreme Court Act 1981)

29.   Offences
In addition to his liability in a civil action for infringement, a person dealing with infringing copies of a work may also commit a criminal offence. Thus –

(a) A person who –

   (i)   makes for sale or hire,

   (ii) imports, otherwise than for his private and domestic use,

   (iii) trades in, or

   (iv) possesses in the course of business, with a view to committing an infringement,

an article which is and which he knows or has reason to believe is, an infringing copy of a protected work, is guilty of an offence; (s.107(1))

(b) A person who makes an article specifically designed or adapted for copying a particular protected work, or has such an article in his possession, is guilty of an offence if he knows that the article is to be used for making infringing copies for commercial purposes; (s.107(2))

(c) A person who causes a literary, dramatic or musical work or a sound recording or film to be played or shown in public knowing or having reason to believe that the playing or showing would infringe copyright in the work, is guilty of an offence. (s.107(3))

(d) A person who dishonestly receives a broadcast or cable programme transmitted from the United Kingdom with intent to avoid payment due on reception of the programme, is guilty of an offence. (s.297)

30.   Local Weights and Measures Authorities
      It is the duty of every local weights and measures authority to enforce
      the provisions of section 107 of the 1988 Act. (s.107A; s.165(2) of
      Criminal Justice and Public Order Act 1994; as at 31 December 1997
      this provision had not been brought into force)

31.   Customs controls
      (a) The owner of the copyright in a published literary, dramatic or
          musical work may request the Commissioners of Customs and
          Excise to treat as prohibited goods printed copies of the work which
          are infringing copies.
      (b) The owner of the copyright in a sound recording or film may request
          the Commissioners to treat as prohibited goods infringing copies of
          the recording or film which the owner expects to arrive in the United
          Kingdom at a specified time and place.
      (c) The Commissioners may only exercise these powers in respect of
          infringing copies arriving –
          (i) from outside the EEA, or
          (ii) from within that area, being copies which have not been entered
               for free circulation.
      (d) The Commissioners may make regulations governing the procedure,
          prescribing forms, fixing fees or imposing conditions relating to the
          exercise of this power. (s.111)

Transition

32.   Schedule 1 to the 1988 Act contains a code of transitional provisions
      which are quite complicated, and this Guide does not attempt to present
      their effect. However, as the 1988 Act made many changes in the law,
      the transitional provisions are important and need to be consulted in
      any case where a problem or dispute arises which involves a pre-1988
      Act factor, for example –
      (a) the institution of legal proceedings in respect of acts which took place
          before the 1988 Act came into force;
      (b) the ownership of rights in a work which was in existence before
          August 1989 in the case where, under the new Act there are new
          provisions relating to authorship e.g. in the case of photographs;
      (c) the subsistence, and enforceability, of moral rights in works which
          were in existence before the new Act came into force;
      (d) the ownership of new rights e.g. rental rights, in works which were
          in existence before the new Act and were the subject of contracts
          made before the Act.

The foregoing instances are not intended to be comprehensive but simply indicative of the kind of questions which may bring the transitional rules into play.

International Arrangements

33.1   There is no such thing as international copyright; copyright is a national right subsisting in a country by virtue of the national law of that country; and national laws are enacted to protect, in the first instance, works of national origin i.e. works by national authors or works first published in the country. However, during the last century it became obvious that the growing traffic in persons, ideas and goods between countries brought about by the steamship, the telegraph and the technical applications of the industrial revolution, was creating growing markets in other countries for literature, drama and music produced within any given country. And it was equally obvious that the benefits of these new markets could not be enjoyed unless the rights and interests of the authors and their publishers who produced and disseminated these works could be protected in countries other than the country of origin.

33.2   This led, at first, to the negotiation of a series of bilateral treaties between countries under which each pair of signatory countries undertook to grant protection to each other's works. Towards the end of the nineteenth century, however, it became apparent that this web of bilateral treaties was creating an increasingly complicated international copyright situation. In consequence, in 1886, the Berne Union was established to create a multilateral copyright treaty to replace the existing proliferation of bilateral treaties.

33.3   The Berne Convention has two principal purposes; first, it stipulates a set of minimum standards of copyright protection which the national copyright laws of member states must provide. Second, it imposes on each member state an obligation to grant to the works of the nationals of, and to the works first published in, every other member state the same protection as the national law extends to its own national works. This is known as the principle of national treatment.

33.4   The Berne Convention has been revised six times and at 31 January 1998, 130 countries were members.

33.5 Until 1 March 1989, the United States of America was not a member of Berne because its copyright law did not conform to the requirements of Berne in several respects, of which the most important were –

(a) the duration of protection under the US law was (until 1 July 1978) two consecutive periods (each of 28 years) running from first publication; whereas the general Berne rule is that the period of protection is the life of the author plus a minimum specified number of years afterwards (which today is 50 years);

(b) under the US law protection was (until 1 January 1989) conditional upon compliance with certain formalities, such as deposit of copies and registration; whereas the Berne Convention expressly requires that copyright should not depend upon formalities.

33.6 As the importance of the US market for copyright works from other countries grew as the 20th century progressed, and equally as American works became increasingly used in foreign markets, it became clear that a multilateral convention providing copyright relations between the USA and other countries was needed; and this was one of the main reasons for the establishment in 1952 of the Universal Copyright Convention.

33.7 This Convention has much the same objectives as Berne, but because it had to accommodate two different copyright systems, its requirements are less specific, and the standard of protection stipulated is much lower than the requirements of Berne. One important provision of the UCC is Article III(1) which stipulates that any provision in the law of a Member State which requires compliance with formalities such as registration or deposit of copies is deemed to be fulfilled if each copy of a work carries a copyright notice in the form of © with the name of the copyright owner and year of first publication.

33.8 The Universal Copyright Convention has been revised once; at 1 April 1998, 98 countries were members, of which 87 are also members of Berne. There are 11 countries which belong only to UCC and 41 which belong only to Berne.

33.9 There are also three other multilateral conventions dealing exclusively with copyright or related rights –

(a) the Rome Convention for the protection of performers, producers of phonograms and broadcasting organisations (1960; membership as at 31 January 1998: 56);

(b) the Geneva Convention for the protection of producers of phonograms against unauthorised duplication of their phonograms (1971; membership as at 31 January 1998: 56);

(c) the Brussels Convention relating to the distribution of programme–carrying signals transmitted by satellite (1974; membership as at 31 January 1998: 22).

33.10   Perhaps the most important additional multilateral agreement dealing, inter alia, with copyright and related rights is that which established the World Trade Organisation with effect from 1 January 1995. The WTO Agreement has a number of associated agreements one of which is the Agreement on Trade–Related Aspects of Intellectual Property Rights, Including Trade in Counterfeit Goods (TRIPS). TRIPS does the following three things –

(a) It sets minimum standards for copyright and related rights; in the case of copyright it requires all member states to comply with Articles 1 - 21 of the Berne Convention (other than Article 6bis which deals with moral rights); in the case of related rights it prescribes a limited set of rights which member states must provide for performers, producers of phonograms and broadcasters.

(b) It contains a detailed code of enforcement measures, procedures and practices which member states must provide.

(c) It establishes a procedure for dealing with complaints that member states are not meeting their copyright and related rights obligations; and for imposing, as a last resort, trading sanctions on member states whose laws have been found not to be in compliance with their obligations and have failed to take steps to rectify the position.

As at 22 October 1997 132 states had joined WTO and an additional 34 had observer status. The general rule is that states must meet their obligations under TRIPS within one year after accession or ratification; but –

(i) developing countries have a further four years within which to bring their laws and practices into line with the TRIPS requirements; and

(ii) least developed countries have an additional five years (i.e. a total of nine years after the end of the initial year).

33.11   It should also be mentioned that in December 1996 in Geneva a Diplomatic Conference adopted the texts of two new treaties –

1. The WIPO Copyright Treaty 1996
2. The WIPO Performers and Phonograms Treaty 1996.

33.12   The purpose of Treaty 1 is to clarify certain Berne rules and establish new provisions which take account of the impact of technology on copyright protection. The purpose of Treaty 2 is to replace the limited international regime of protection for performers and phonogram producers contained in the Rome Convention by an up to date regime which takes account of contemporary needs, including, in particular, the impact of technology.

33.13   Neither treaty will come into force until it has been ratified or acceded to by 30 states. The United Kingdom was one of the signatories to both treaties in Geneva, and is expected in due course to ratify them both. It is likely that the necessary accessions and ratifications will have been received by the end of 1998; and this will mean that the law in the United Kingdom will have been, or will have to be, amended in important ways, particularly in relation to performers' rights. As soon as this occurs the BCC hopes to publish a supplement to this Guide summarizing the effects of those amendments.

33.14   Pursuant to these various international agreements (other than the Brussels Convention of which the United Kingdom is not a member), the United Kingdom has applied the provisions of the UK copyright law to works originating in the other member states which are parties to these agreements. In the result, therefore, works originating in most other countries are also protected in the United Kingdom under the 1988 Act in the same way as works originating in the United Kingdom are protected. In certain cases, however, the ambit of protection is reduced so as to correspond to the protection given in a particular country to United Kingdom works; for example, sound recordings originating in the United States are protected in the United Kingdom under the 1988 Act but that protection does not include the rights of public performance, broadcasting or cable distribution because under the copyright law of the United States, sound recordings, including those originating in the United Kingdom, do not enjoy those rights. In order to determine whether a work originating in another country is protected under UK law and, if it is, the extent of the protection, it is always necessary to consult the current Copyright (Application to Other Countries) Order made under section 159 of the 1988 Act.

The Administration of Copyright

Assignments and licences

34.1   Copyright is a form of property; it can be sold, leased, given away or bequeathed, like other forms of property. (s.90(1)) If ownership of copyright is to be transferred from one person to another, the assignment must be in writing (s.90(3)), and so must an exclusive licence which has almost the same effect as an assignment (s.92(2)); but if the copyright owner intends simply to give another person permission to use his copyright, the licence (other than an exclusive licence) may take any form; it may be in writing or it may be oral; or it may be inferred from conduct. In practice, it is desirable in order to remove doubt and avoid subsequent dispute, that licences should be in writing.

34.2   Both assignments and licences may be limited in various ways; an assignment or a licence may deal with the copyright subsisting under the law of one country only or of several countries; thus, an author may assign his UK copyright to one person and his American copyright to another, and so on; and similarly with licences.

34.3   Licences may be exclusive or non-exclusive; and both assignments and licences may be made in respect of one or more of the component parts of copyright (s.90(2)(a)); thus an author may assign the publishing right in his work to one person, the broadcasting right to another, and may simply grant a non-exclusive licence to a third person in respect of the public performance right. Assignments and licences may be limited to a part only of the full duration of the copyright period. (s.90(2)(b))

34.4   Exclusive licensees
        Subject to certain special rules regarding infringement actions, exclusive licensees have, except against the copyright owner, the same rights and remedies as if the licence had been an assignment. (ss.101,102)

34.5   Presumption of transfer in films
        In a film production agreement between a producer and an author, the author is presumed to have transferred his rental right in the film to the producer, unless the agreement states otherwise. This presumption does not apply to the rental rights of the author of the screenplay or of the dialogue or of any music specifically created for and used in the film. (s.93A)

55

34.6   Transfer of rental right - equitable remuneration
Where an author transfers, or is presumed to have transferred, his rental
right in respect of a sound recording or film to the producer he retains
a right to equitable remuneration, which cannot be excluded or
restricted by contract. The remuneration is payable by the producer or
his successor in title; and in the absence of agreement the amount is fixed
by the Copyright Tribunal. Remuneration is not inequitable simply
because it takes the form of a single payment made at the time of the
transfer. (ss.93B, 93C)

34.7   Future copyright
The copyright which may come into existence when a work is created
in the future or on the occurrence of a future event may be the subject
of an assignment or licence. (s.91)

Individual administration

34.8   Copyright is an individual right subsisting in an individual work and at
its inception belonging normally to the author (subject to the exceptions
set out in para. 8.3 above). Because authors, composers and artists are
not usually businessmen, in most cases they entrust the administration
of their rights of copyright to others who have the managerial and
entrepreneurial experience and expertise needed to obtain the best
commercial results.

34.9   In the literary field an author may entrust his rights directly to a
publisher. Alternatively, he may use a literary agent to negotiate his
contract with the publisher and oversee the implementation of the
contract on his behalf; or to procure the commercial exploitation of
rights not granted to the publisher. Also available to authors are the
services of various unions and similar bodies which seek to protect the
interests of their members in various ways, including the negotiation of
standard or minimum terms for the use of their copyright, e.g. the Society
of Authors, the Writers Guild, the National Union of Journalists and
others - see full list in Appendix 6. Recent years have seen the growth
of collective administration of copyright principally in the case of literary
works, to meet the needs of modern technology such as photocopying
(see para 34.11 below). In practice, anyone wishing to make use of a
published literary work protected by copyright should, in the first
instance, apply to the author's agent, if known, and if not, to the
publisher.

Collective administration

34.10   Where the volume of a particular form of use of a particular category of work is very high and takes place at a multiplicity of venues and the selection of the individual works to be used is frequently made immediately before use, individual administration by the issue of individual licences by each right owner in respect of each work used is impractical. The classic example is the public performance of music. In the middle of the last century it was recognised - in France - that the public performance of music, in halls, restaurants, cafes and a multitude of other places could not possibly be licensed by either the composers or their publishers on an individual basis; and the first composers' society was established - SACEM. To-day such societies exist in almost all countries where there is a copyright system; and they administer various categories of rights. Collective administration bodies benefit the users as well as the right owners. It would not only be extremely burdensome and costly for a broadcaster, for example, to discharge its copyright obligations by seeking out the copyright owner of each musical work which it transmits, in advance of transmission, and obtaining an individual licence, but quite impossible in practice. By obtaining a blanket licence, which is usually issued on an annual rolling over basis, the broadcaster can obtain permission to transmit all or any musical work in virtually the world's repertoire of copyright music.

34.11   In the literary field, The Authors' Licensing and Collecting Society (ALCS) was established by authors to administer collectively certain rights in literary and dramatic works, which could no longer be effectively administered on an individual basis. Among these are –
(a) the right to make copies by the use of reprographic equipment;
(b) the right to make copies of works by recording them when received "off-air" in radio or television programmes; and
(c) the right to include works in a cable programme service by immediate onward transmission of radio or television programmes containing those works.

Publishers have also established a body for collectively administering their interests in the copying of literary works by means of reprography – The Publishers Licensing Society (PLS); and ALCS and PLS have jointly established the Copyright Licensing Agency (CLA) for the purpose of licensing the reprographic copying of literary works by issuing blanket licences covering copying by institutions both in the public and private sector. So far, licensing schemes are in operation covering photocopying in most primary and secondary schools, polytechnics and universities; and the licensing of photocopying in government institutions and in industry and commerce is well advanced. The 1988 Act defines reprography as a process for making facsimile copies, or involving the use of an appliance for making multiple copies. (s.178)

34.12 Similar blanket licences are available under a licensing scheme promulgated by the Educational Recording Agency Ltd (ERA) set up by the broadcasters, ALCS, the Mechanical Copyright Protection Society (MCPS), the Design and Artists Copyright Society (DACS) and other smaller groups of right holders. These licences are available to educational establishments and cover the recording off–air of protected material in broadcasts and cable programmes for the purpose of educational instruction. For the purposes of the Act, an educational establishment is –
(a) any school as defined in the Education Acts relating to England, Wales, Scotland and Northern Ireland, or
(b) any other educational establishment specified for the purposes of the Act by the Secretary of State. (s.174(1)-(4))

34.13 In the case of music the normal arrangement is for the composer to assign his copyright to a publisher for commercial exploitation and administration subject, however, to the services provided by the Performing Right Society (PRS) and the Mechanical Copyright Protection Society (MCPS).

34.14 In the field of music the public performance, broadcasting and cable distribution rights are usually referred to jointly as "performing rights" and, in the United Kingdom, have been collectively administered since the beginning of the century. "Performing rights" are almost exclusively administered by the PRS, to whom application should be made by anyone wishing to perform a musical work in public or broadcast it or include it in a cable programme service.

34.15 The right to record music onto discs or tapes is often referred to as the "mechanical right"; the right to incorporate music in the sound-track of a film is known as the "synchronization right"; each of these rights may be administered either by MCPS or by the music publisher. In practice application for a licence may be made to MCPS and, if MCPS does not administer the rights in a particular case, it will advise to whom application should be made.

34.16   From 1998 PRS and MCPS, though remaining separate legal entities, will be jointly administered by a single senior management team housed in the offices previously occupied exclusively by PRS; and they describe their joint relationship as the Music Alliance.

34.17   The rights in sound recordings are generally administered by the individual record producers, save that the public performance, broadcasting and cable distribution rights are collectively administered by Phonographic Performance Limited (PPL) on behalf of the producers; and an affiliated body, Video Performance Limited (VPL) administers collectively those rights in music videos.

34.18   The film industry operates primarily on the basis of the individual administration of rights in individual films.

34.19   In the field of artistic works, the Design and Artists Copyright Society (DACS) was established to license, on behalf of artists, the reproduction of artistic works in any medium. There are also a number of unions representing artists, photographers and other creative groups. Up to now the actual business of administering rights has normally been carried out by the individual right owners, but increasing use is being made of collective administration.

34.20   Collective anti-piracy operations
In the face of widescale piracy some groups of copyright owners have established organisations with specific responsibility for enforcing rights against pirates. These organisations do not license users; they carry out a purely enforcement function by seeking and collecting evidence of piracy and bringing legal proceedings, usually criminal prosecutions, against infringers. The Federation Against Software Theft (FAST) carries out this work on behalf of computer program producers; and the Federation Against Copyright Theft (FACT) performs a similar function for the film industy.

SECTION II - RIGHTS IN PERFORMANCES

Background

<u>Before 1 August 1989</u>

35.1 Prior to the 1988 Act, "performances" enjoyed a form of protection under the Performers' Protection Acts 1958-1972. The salient features of that protection were the following –

(a) It was directed at protecting the interests of performers only.

(b) Performers, for the purposes of the legislation, were those who act, sing, play or otherwise perform literary, dramatic, musical or artistic works; thus linking the protection to performances only of the works which are protected under the law of copyright.

(c) The protection granted was by way of penal provisions i.e. by the creation of offences which would be committed by persons who carried out certain acts in relation to performances without the consent of the performer.

<u>1 August 1989 - 30 November 1996</u>

35.2 Part II and Schedule 2 of the 1988 Act completely repealed and replaced the Performers' Protection Acts 1958-1972 and introduced a new code with the following principal features –

(a) The protection under the 1988 Act is concerned with the interests not only of performers but also of persons who have "recording rights in relation to the performance" which, in effect, means principally film and record producers. (s.180(1))

(b) The performances protected by the new law are not limited to performances of works protected by copyright, but include performances of variety acts and similar presentations. (s.180(2))

(c) Under the 1988 Act, performers and persons having recording rights are not given rights in the nature of copyright i.e. property rights which may be assigned or licensed in the same way as rights of copyright may be dealt with; but the law does give them civil rights of action, with a full range of remedies, which they may bring when performances in which they have an interest are used in various ways without their consent.

(d) In addition to the right to bring civil proceedings, penal provisions corresponding to offences under the old law are included in the 1988 Act. (ss.180(1), 198 and 201)

From 1 December 1996

35.3   The Copyright and Related Rights Regulations 1996, which came into force on 1 December 1996, amended the 1988 Act to implement the EU Rental Directive by providing additional protection for performers, the principal features of which are –
(a) Four new rights are conferred on performers –
    (i) a reproduction right,
    (ii) a distribution right,
    (iii) a rental right, and
    (iv) a lending right.
(b) These rights are expressly declared to be "property rights".
(s.191A)

35.4   Under the current law, therefore, there are two separate regimes of protection applying to performances –

A. The regime established by the 1988 Act as originally enacted, under which the rights of performers and persons having recording rights are now expressly referred to as "non property rights" and are declared not to be assignable or transmissible. (ss. 192A(1), 192B(1))

B. The regime established by the 1996 amendments under which the new rights are property rights the exercise of which are, generally, subject to the same rules as apply to the rights of copyright described in Section I of this Guide.

Territorial Application of the Law Relating to Performances

36.1   Part II of the 1988 Act (relating to performances) applies to anything done in –
(a) England, Wales, Scotland and Northern Ireland;
(b) the territorial waters of the United Kingdom, and the UK sector of the continental shelf;
(c) ships, aircraft and hovercraft registered in the United Kingdom.
(ss. 207, 209, 210)

36.2   Part II may also, by Order in Council, –
(a) be extended to
    (i)   any of the Channel Islands,
    (ii)   the Isle of Man,

(iii) any colony;

(b) be applied to any foreign country. (s.208)

Application to Past Performances

37. Part II of the 1988 Act applies to performances which took place before the commencement of the Act or, in the case of a new right established by the 1996 amendments, before the commencement of the 1996 Regulations, as well as to subsequent performances, but nothing done before the Act, or the Regulations, as the case may be, came into force may be treated as an infringement of any of the rights created by the Act, or by the amendments to the Act made by the Regulations. (s.180(3); Reg.26)

Conditions for Protection

38.1 To qualify for performers' rights –
(a) the performer must be a citizen, subject or resident of –
(i) the United Kingdom, or
(ii) any other EEC country, or
(iii) a country designated under the Act as enjoying reciprocal protection;
or
(b) the performance must take place in a qualifying country i.e. one of those mentioned in sub-paragraphs (i)-(iii) above. (ss.181, 206)

The national origin of the material performed is irrelevant; provided either the performer is a qualifying individual, or the performance takes place in a qualifying country, the performance will be protected.

38.2 To qualify for recording rights, a person must –
(a) be a qualifying person i.e.–
(i) an individual who meets one of the qualifications set out in sub-paragraph 38.1(a) above; or
(ii) a corporate body formed under the law of the United Kingdom or of another qualifying country, and which carries on substantial business in such a country; and
(b) have acquired exclusive recording rights over a performance by way of an assignment or an exclusive licence. (ss.185, 206)

38.3 It is to be noted that provided a person is a qualifying person (which includes both individuals and corporate bodies), he may acquire recording rights even if the performance is not a qualifying performance.

Thus, a United Kingdom company may acquire recording rights, enforceable in the United Kingdom, in respect of a performance in the United States of America by a Brazilian performer.

A. Regime of Non-Property Rights

Performers' Rights

39.   The acts which infringe a performers' non-property rights in a qualifying performance are, without the performer's consent, –

(a) making, otherwise than for private and domestic use, a recording directly from a live performance by him; (s.182(1)(a))

(b) broadcasting his performance live, or including it live in a cable programme service; (s.182(1)(b))

(c) making, otherwise than for private and domestic use, a recording directly from a broadcast of, or cable programme including, his live performance; (s.182(1)(c))

(d) using a recording, known to have been made without the performer's consent, to broadcast, include in a cable service, or give a public performance of, his performance; (s.183)

(e) otherwise than for private and domestic use, importing, or trading in, the recording of a performance known to have been made without the consent of the performer. (s.184)

Recording Rights

40.   The rights of a person having recording rights are similar, but not identical to a performer's rights. Thus, the rights of a person having rights in relation to a performance are infringed by someone who does any of the following acts –

(a) makes, otherwise than for private and domestic use, a recording of the performance, without the consent of the person having recording rights, or the consent of the performer; (s.186(1))

(b) presents in public, broadcasts or includes in a cable programme service, a recording of a performance, without

(i) the consent of the person having recording rights, or

(ii) if the performance was a qualifying one, the consent of the performer,

if the person responsible for the public presentation, broadcast or cable use knew, or had reason to believe, that the making of the recording had not been authorised; (s.187)

(c) imports or trades in, the recording of a performance, the making of which is known not to have been authorised. (s.188)

Infringement of Non-Property Rights

41.　An infringement of the non-property rights of a performer or of a person having recording rights takes place if the infringing act is committed in relation to the whole or a substantial part of the performance. (ss.182(1), 186(1))

Transmission of Non-Property Rights

42.　The Act declares that non-property rights are not assignable or transmissible, save that –

(a) a person entitled to performers' rights may by will specifically direct that some designated person may exercise the rights;

(b) and, if there is no such direction, the rights may be exercised by his personal representatives. (ss.192A(1)),192B(1))

Enforcement of Non-Property Rights

43.1　An infringement of the non-property rights of a performer and of a person having recording rights is actionable as a breach of statutory duty. (s.194)

43.2　In addition, the following special remedies may be invoked –

(a) a person entitled to non-property rights may apply to the court for an order that any illicit recordings in the possession of someone in the course of business be delivered up; (s.195)

(b) where a person entitled to non-property rights finds illicit recordings exposed or otherwise available for sale or hire in circumstances which would justify him applying for an order under sub–paragraph (a), he may seize the recordings, subject to certain safeguards i.e. advance notice of the proposed seizure must be given to the police;

only premises to which the public have access may be entered; and force may not be used. (s.196)

B. Regime of Property Rights

44.1 The acts which infringe a performer's property rights in a qualifying performance are, without the performer's consent, –

(a) making, otherwise than for private and domestic use, either directly or indirectly, a copy of a recording of his performance; (s.182A - the reproduction right)

(b) issuing to the public copies of a recording of his performance; this means –

(i) the act of putting into circulation in the EEA copies not previously put into circulation in the EEA by or with the consent of the performer; or

(ii) the act of putting into circulation outside the EEA copies not previously put into circulation in the EEA or elsewhere; but does not include –

(iii) any subsequent distribution, sale, hiring or loan of copies previously put into circulation; or

(iv) any subsequent importation of such copies into the United Kingdom or another EEA state;

but (iii) and (iv) do not affect the exercise of the rental and lending rights or the right to control the circulation within (including importation into) the EEA of copies not previously circulated in the EEA with the consent of the performer; (s.182B - the distribution right)

(c) making a copy of a recording of his performance available for use on terms that it will or may be returned, for direct or indirect commercial or economic advantage; (s.182C(1)(2)(a) – the rental right)

(d) making a copy of a recording of his performance available for use, on terms that it will or may be returned, otherwise than for direct or indirect economic or commercial advantage, through an establishment which is accessible to the public. (s.182C(1)(2)(b)) – the lending right)

44.2 "Rental" and "lending" do not include –

(a) making available for the purpose of public performance, playing or showing in public, broadcasting or inclusion in a cable programme service;

(b) making available for the purpose of exhibition in public;

65

(c) making available for on-the-spot reference use; and "lending" does not include making available between establishments which are accessible to the public. (s.182C(3)(4))

Equitable Remuneration for Broadcast, Cable Use or Public Playing of Recordings

45.1   Where a commercially published sound recording of a qualifying performance is broadcast or included in a cable programme service, or is played in public, the performer is entitled to equitable remuneration from the owner of the copyright in the recording. (s.182D(1))

45.2   In the absence of agreement the amount of the equitable remuneration is determined by the Copyright Tribunal. (s.182D(3)(4)(5)(6))

45.3   The right to equitable remuneration may not be assigned by the performer save to a collecting society; but it may be transmitted by will or by operation of law as personal or moveable property; and it may be further assigned or transmitted by any person to whom it passes. (s.182D(2))

45.4   Any agreement which purports to exclude or restrict the right or prevent its evaluation by the Tribunal is of no effect. (s.182D(7))

Property Rights Subject to Provisions Corresponding to Copyright Provisions

46.   In relation to the following matters the performer's property rights are subject to provisions corresponding to provisions to which rights of copyright are subject –
Assignments and licences – see paras. 34.1-34.3 (s.191B)
Future rights – see para. 34.7 (s.191C)
Exclusive licensees – see paras. 28.1, 28.2, 34.4 (ss.191D, 191L, 191M)
Bequest of a recording of a performance – see para. 8.5 (s.181E)
Presumption of transfer – see para. 34.5 (s.191F)
Transfer of rental right – equitable remuneration – see para. 34.6 (ss.191G, 191H)
Infringement actions – see para. 28 (s.191I)
Powers of seizure of illicit recordings – see para. 28.4 (ss.195, 196, 203, 204, 205)
Offences – see para. 29(a)(c) (s.198(1)(2))
Exceptions – see paras. 13.1-13.2.34 (s.189, Sch.2)

Illicit Recordings

47.1 In the case of performers' rights, a recording is illicit if it is made, otherwise than for private purposes, of the whole or a substantial part of a performance without the performer's consent. (s.197(2))

47.2 In the case of a person having recording rights, a recording is illicit if it is made, otherwise than for private purposes, of the whole or a substantial part of a performance, without either the consent of the person having recording rights, or the consent of the performer. (s.197(3))

Duration – Applicable to Both Non-Property and Property Rights

48.1 All rights in relation to a performance (ie. both non-property and property rights) expire –
(a) 50 years after the end of the year in which the performance took place, but
(b) if during that period a recording of the performance is released, 50 years after the end of the year of release. (s.191(2))

48.2 "Released" means
(i) first published,
(ii) first played or shown in public,
(iii) first broadcast,
(iv) first included in a cable programme service,
provided in all cases that the act of release was authorised. (s.191(3); see para. 7.5(b) above)

48.3 Where the performer is not a national of an EEA State the duration of rights under the Act is that to which the performance is entitled in the country of which he is a national, but must not exceed the duration which would apply under para.48.1 above, unless this restriction would be contrary to an international agreement entered into by the United Kingdom prior to 29 October 1993, in which case para.48.1 will apply. (s.191(4)(5); see para.7.5(c) above)

The Copyright Tribunal

49.1   Jurisdiction over performers' property rights
        In the case of the property rights in performances, the Tribunal has
        jurisdiction over licensing schemes and licences from licensing bodies
        which corresponds to the Tribunal's jurisdiction over licensing schemes
        and licences from licensing bodies in the case of copyright – see
        paras.17.1, 17.2, 18.1, 18.2, 18.3. (s.205A, Sch.2A)

49.2   Other jurisdiction
        The Tribunal also has jurisdiction over the following matters –
        (a) determining the equitable remuneration in respect of the public use
            of a commercially published sound recording, under s.182D;
        (b) granting consent for the exercise of the reproduction right when the
            right owner cannot be ascertained, under s.190;
        (c) determining the equitable remuneration when the rental right is
            transferred, under s.191H;
        (d) determination of payment due in respect of the retransmission of
            broadcasts containing performances or recordings, under para.19 of
            Sch.2. (s.205B(1)(a)(b)(c)(cc))

SECTION III - FINAL OBSERVATIONS

General Caveat

50.   Copyright, including rights in performances, is a specialised field of law; the general principles are subject to numerous and often complex exceptions and qualifications; the copyright and performance rights provisions of the Copyright, Designs and Patents Act 1988 changed the law in many respects, and introduced new concepts and provisions. The 1988 Act itself has now been substantially amended, principally to meet the requirements of various EU Directives, the objectives of which have been twofold. First there is the overall objective to bring about harmonization of the laws of the member states of the European Union; and second, the need to ensure that the laws of member states adequately take account of contemporary circumstances, notably the impact on the copyright system of technology, especially the technique of digitalization.

The Impact of Technology

51.   The impact of technology on the copyright system has been large and spectacular; and it is a continuing process; new technologies, new applications appear almost daily; today's marvels are out of date tomorrow. Technology has affected the copyright system in various important ways.

51.1   New kinds of works

It has led to new forms of creativity, resulting in new kinds of works protected by the system; the best example is the computer program.

51.2   New forms of use

It has generated new forms of use and methods of dissemination; such as satellite broadcasting, the perfect reproduction quality of digital CD recordings, the interactive communication systems which enable an individual member of the public to select what he wants to hear or see, and when, and to himself activate the communication of the selected material to his home speaker or screen – systems which many think may replace retail sales of material objects such as books and discs as the normal method by which the public in the future will acquire the literature, drama, music and information it wishes to have access to.

69

51.3   Global markets

One of the important consequences of these developments is that the public addressed by the author, publisher or producer is no longer the public of a particular country or region; the market for intellectual property is worldwide.

51.4   Increased volume of use

Another consequence of technology has been the growth in the volume of use. Because of the scope for worldwide dissemination and the enormous capacity of modern communication systems using digital and compression and other techniques the dimensions of the use today of protected works are exponentially greater than the levels in the middle of the century.

51.5   Effective licensing

One of the major challenges created by the contemporary technological environment is the need for effective arrangements which ensure that this huge volume of use is properly authorised, monitored and paid for. Increased use of collective administration may help in certain cases, at least in the short term; but looking ahead, it may be that technology itself may produce the solutions, possibly by imbedding in works electronic signals carrying information about the copyright status of the work, its ownership and the approved licensing terms for its use, which would be read by devices incorporated in the transmitting, receiving or recording equipment involved in the distribution and final consumption of the works.

The Contemporary Scene

52.1   The salient feature of the scenario briefly sketched above is that the copyright system is in a state of evolution and flux. Much of the legislation has not been considered by the courts; new business practices are being negotiated to accommodate current conditions; and new arrangements, administrative and technical, are being devised to ensure adequate protection for right owners and adequate access for users.

52.2   The purpose of this Guide is not to attempt to provide specific answers or advice on particular questions, but simply to indicate to creative people what rights they may have and what interests they may need to safeguard; and to alert users of literary, dramatic, musical, artistic and other works and performances protected by the law of copyright in the United Kingdom to what their responsibilities may be.

Appendices

53.1   There are 6 accompanying appendices –
1. Legislation
2. Territories and countries to which the Act has been extended or applied
3. Conventions
4. Qualifying broadcasting services
5. Information about the British Copyright Council
6. Organisations involved in the administration of copyright and rights in performances.

53.2   The information in the Appendices reflects the position as at 31 December 1997. As that date recedes it becomes important to check that changes have not taken place. In the case of subsidiary legislation and countries to which the law has been extended, enquiries may be addressed to the Copyright Directorate, The Patent Office, 25 Southampton Buildings, London WC2A 1AY.
Tel: 0171 438 4777; Fax: 0171 438 4713;
E-mail: copyright@patent.gov.uk; Website: www.patent.gov.uk

APPENDIX 1

The UK Legislation

The Copyright, Designs and Patents Act 1988 (c. 48) as amended by –

The Broadcasting Act 1990

The Copyright (Computer) Regulations 1992

The Judicial Pensions and Retirement Act 1993

The Trade Marks Act 1994

The Criminal Justice and Public Order Act 1994

The Criminal Justice (Northern Ireland) Order 1994

The Merchant Shipping Act 1995

The Duration of Copyright and Rights in Performances Regulations 1995

The Copyright (EC Measures Relating to Pirated Goods and Abolition of Restriction on the Import of Goods) Regulations 1995

The Broadcasting Act 1996

The Copyright and Related Rights Regulations 1996

The Copyright and Rights in Databases Regulations 1997

The European Union Directives

Directive of 14 May 1991 on the legal protection of computer software (91/250/EEC)

Directive of 19 November 1992 on rental right and lending right and on certain rights related to copyright in the field of intellectual property (92/100/EEC)

Directive of 27 September 1993 on the coordination of certain rules concerning copyright and rights related to copyright applicable to satellite broadcasting and cable retransmission (93/83/EEC)

Directive of 29 October 1993 harmonizing the term of protection of copyright and certain related rights (93/98/EEC)

Directive of 11 March 1996 on the legal protection of databases (96/9/EC)

APPENDIX 2

A. *Countries and Territories to which Part I of the Act (dealing with copyright) has been applied*

Part 1 – in relation to all works except broadcasts and cable programmes

Algeria
Andorra
Antigua and Barbuda
Argentina
Australia
Austria
Bahamas
Bahrain
Bangladesh
Barbados
Belgium
Belize
Benin
Bolivia
Botswana
Brazil
Brunei Darussalam
Bulgaria
Burkina Faso
Burundi
Cameroon
Canada
Central African Republic
Chad
Chile
China
Colombia
Congo
Costa Rica
Cote d'Ivoire
Croatia
Cuba
Cyprus
Czech Republic
Denmark

Djibouti
Dominica
Dominican Republic
Ecuador
Egypt
El Salvador
Fiji
Finland
France
Gabon
Gambia
Germany
Ghana
Greece
Guatemala
Guinea
Guinea-Bissau
Haiti
Holy See
Honduras
Hungary
Iceland
India
Ireland
Israel
Italy
Japan
Kampuchea
Kenya
Korea, Republic of
Kuwait
Laos
Lebanon
Lesotho
Liberia

Libya
Liechtenstein
Luxembourg
Macao
Madagascar
Malawi
Malaysia
Maldives
Mali
Malta
Mauritania
Mauritius
Mexico
Monaco
Morocco
Mozambique
Myanmar
Netherlands
New Zealand
Nicaragua
Niger
Nigeria
Norway
Pakistan
Panama
Paraguay
Peru
Philippines
Poland
Portugal

Romania
Rwanda
St. Vincent and the
Grenadines
Senegal
Sierra Leone
Singapore
Slovenia
South Africa
Soviet Union
Spain
Sri Lanka
Suriname
Swaziland
Sweden
Switzerland
Thailand
Togo
Trinidad and Tobago
Tunisia
Turkey
Uganda
United States of America
Uruguay
Venezuela
Yugoslavia
Zaire
Zambia
Zimbabwe

Part 2 - in relation to sound recordings which enjoy full protection

Argentina
Australia
Austria
Bangladesh
Barbados
Brazil
Burkina Faso
Chile
Colombia

Congo
Costa Rica
Czechoslovakia
Denmark
Dominican Republic
Ecuador
El Salvador
Fiji
Finland

France
Germany
Ghana
Greece
Guatemala
Honduras
India
Indonesia
Ireland
Italy
Japan
Lesotho

Luxembourg
Malawi
Malaysia
Mexico
Monaco
New Zealand
Niger
Norway
Pakistan
Panama
Paraguay
Peru

Part 3 - in relation to broadcasts

Antigua and Barbuda
Argentina
Australia
Austria
Bahrain
Bangladesh
Barbados
Belgium
Belize
Bolivia
Botswana
Brazil
Brunei Darussalam
Burkina Faso
Burundi
Canada
Central African Republic
Chile
Colombia
Congo
Costa Rica
Cote d'Ivoire
Cuba
Cyprus
Czech Republic
Denmark
Djibouti

Dominica
Dominican Republic
Ecuador
Egypt
El Salvador
Fiji
Finland
France
Gabon
Germany
Ghana
Greece
Guatemala
Guinea-Bissau
Guinea
Guyana
India
Ireland
Israel
Japan
Kenya
Korea, Republic of
Kuwait
Lesotho
Liechtenstein
Luxembourg
Macao

Malawi
Malaysia
Maldives
Mali
Malta
Mauritania
Mauritius
Mexico
Monaco
Morocco
Mozambique
Namibia
New Zealand
Nicaragua
Niger
Norway
Pakistan
Panama
Paraguay
Peru
Philippines
Poland
Portugal
Romania
Saint Lucia

Saint Vincent and the
Grenadines
Senegal
Sierra Leone
Singapore
Slovenia
South Africa
Spain
Sri Lanka
Suriname
Swaziland
Sweden
Tanzania
Thailand
Togo
Trinidad and Tobago
Tunisia
Turkey
Uganda
Uruguay
United States of America
Venezuela
Zambia
Zimbabwe

B.   *Countries and Territories enjoying reciprocal protection under Part II of the Act (dealing with rights in performances)*

Part 1 - in respect of all rights in performances provided in Part II of the Act

Argentina
Australia
Barbados
Bolivia
Brazil
Bulgaria
Burkina Faso
Chile
Colombia
Congo
Costa Rica

Czech Republic
Denmark
Dominican Republic
Ecuador
El Salvador
Fiji
Finland
France
Germany
Greece
Guatemala

Honduras
Hungary
Iceland
Ireland
Italy
Jamaica
Japan
Lesotho
Luxembourg
Mexico
Moldova
Monaco
Netherlands

Niger
Nigeria
Norway
Panama
Paraguay
Peru
Philippines
Slovak Republic
Spain
Sweden
Switzerland
Uruguay

<u>Part 2 - in respect only of the following rights –</u>

(a) making a sound recording from a live performance, or a copy of such a recording;
(b) broadcasting a live performance, or including a live performance in a cable programme service.

Antigua and Barbuda
Bahrain
Bangladesh
Belgium
Belize
Botswana
Brunei Darussalam
Burundi
Canada
Central African Republic
Cote d'Ivoire
Cyprus
Djibouti
Dominica
Egypt
Gabon
Ghana
Guinea
Guinea-Bissau
Guyana
Hong Kong

India
Indonesia
Israel
Kenya
Korea, Republic of
Kuwait
Liechtenstein
Macao
Malawi
Malaysia
Maldives
Mali
Malta
Mauritania
Mauritius
Morocco
Mozambique
Myanmar
Namibia
New Zealand
Nicaragua

Pakistan
Poland
Portugal
Saint Lucia
Saint Vincent and the
Grenadines
Senegal
Sierra Leone
Singapore
Slovenia
South Africa
Sri Lanka
Suriname

Swaziland
Tanzania
Thailand
Togo
Trinidad and Tobago
Tunisia
Turkey
Uganda
United States of America
Venezuela
Zambia
Zimbabwe

APPENDIX 3

The Conventions to which the United Kingdom is a Party

1. The Berne Convention (1886) as revised and amended up to 1979

2. The Universal Copyright Convention (1952) as revised in 1971

3. The Rome Convention for the Protection of Performers, Producers of Phonograms and Broadcasting Organisations (1961)

4. The Geneva Convention for the Protection of Producers of Phonograms Against Unauthorised Duplication of Their Phonograms (1971)

5. The World Trade Organisation Associated Agreement on Trade–Related Aspects of Intellectual Property Rights, Including Trade in Counterfeit Goods (TRIPS) (with effect from 1 January 1995)

Conventions Not Yet In Force

The WIPO Copyright Treaty 1996

The WIPO Performers and Phonograms Treaty 1996

The texts of these two treaties were adopted by a Diplomatic Conference in Geneva in December 1996. The United Kingdom is a signatory to both texts, and is expected to ratify both.

APPENDIX 4

Qualifying Services for the Purposes of Section 73 - Para.13.2.9 (Compulsory licence for cable retransmission)

(i) any regional or national Channel 3 service

(ii) Channel 4, Channel 5 and S4C

(iii) the teletext service referred to in section 49(2) of the Broadcasting Act 1990

(iv) the service referred to in section 57(1A)(a) of that Act (power of S4C to provide digital service)

(v) the television broadcasting services and teletext service of the BBC

APPENDIX 5

Information about the British Copyright Council

Purposes

The purposes of the Council are:
(a) to defend and foster the principles of copyright and to encourage their understanding and acceptance throughout the world;
(b) to bring together the bodies who speak for those who create, or hold interests or rights of copyright in literary, dramatic, musical and artistic works and those who perform such works;
(c) to monitor changes in law, in administration, in social practice and in technology which may affect the principles of copyright;
(d) to urge upon the British Government and all appropriate authorities and bodies at home and abroad such advice or action as the Council may decide;
(e) to consider any matter relating to copyright.

Status

The present form of the Council was settled in 1965. It is an association of bodies representing those who create, or hold interests or rights in literary, dramatic, musical and artistic works, and those who give performances, or hold rights or interests in performances, being works and performances in which rights subsist under the Copyright, Designs and Patents Act 1988. The Council is unincorporated, and has no formal constitution.

Officers

The Council's officers are the President, Chairman, Vice Presidents, Vice Chairmen, the Secretary and the Treasurer. They are all unpaid except for the Secretary.

Membership

Applications for membership are considered by the Council at its regular meetings. To be successful, they must receive the general support of the existing members. Each member organisation is entitled to nominate representatives (normally not more than 2) to attend meetings of the Council and receive papers and other information disseminated by the Council.

Finance

The Council receives no grants and relies on the financial support of its membership to finance its activities. Members pay an annual subscription determined by the Council, the level of which varies according to the size of the organisation concerned. The Council's financial year runs from 1st July to 30th June. Accounts are submitted annually to the membership. The Council has been accepted by the Inland Revenue as a non-trading organisation, for tax purposes.

Meetings

Meetings of the Council are held at approximately two-monthly intervals. Matters requiring detailed consideration may be referred to working parties. Twice a year there is a joint meeting with Copyright Directorate of the Patent Office.

APPENDIX 6

The information given below in respect of each of the listed organisations was provided by the organisation concerned.

Organisations involved in the administration of copyright and rights in performances

Table I: Organisations engaged in collective licensing

* Member of the British Copyright Council

*AUTHORS' LICENSING AND COLLECTING SOCIETY
ALCS administers rights for writers in the literary and dramatic fields, where collective administration is particularly effective, covering reprography, cable retransmission, the lending right overseas and off-air and private recording.
Address: Marlborough Court, 14-18 Holborn, London EC1N 2LE.
Tel: 0171 395 0600; Fax: 0171 395 0660;
E-mail: alcs@alcs.co.uk; Website: http://www.alcs.co.uk

COPYRIGHT LICENSING AGENCY
CLA licenses the reprographic copying of literary works, specifically books, journals and periodicals. It issues blanket licences for copying by institutions in education, government, public bodies and commerce and industry. CLA is developing a licence which will permit limited digitisation of literary works.
Address: 90 Tottenham Court Road, London W1P 0LP.
Tel: 0171 436 5931; Fax: 0171 436 3986;
E-mail: cla@cla.co.uk; Website: http://www.cla.co.uk

*DESIGN AND ARTISTS COPYRIGHT SOCIETY
DACS was established in 1983 as the copyright and collecting society for visual artists in the UK. It licences reproductions of its members' works on an individual basis and is also active in the collective administration of reprographic, cable retransmission and off-air recording rights for visual artists. DACS works for the benefit of all creators of artistic works (including photographers) whether British or foreign, famous or unknown.
Address: Parchment House, 13 Northburgh Street, London EC1V 0AH.
Tel: 0171 336 8811; Fax: 0171 336 8822;
E-mail: Info@dacs.co.uk

EDUCATIONAL RECORDING AGENCY

ERA issues licences to educational establishments for recording off-air from broadcast and cable programmes for the purpose of educational instruction.
Address: New Premier House, 150 Southampton Row, London WC1B 5AL.
Tel: 0171 837 3222; Fax: 0171 837 3750;
E-mail: era.era.org.uk

INTERNATIONAL FEDERATION OF PHONOGRAPHIC INDUSTRIES

IFPI licenses public performance, broadcasting and cable distribution rights in certain sound recordings, mainly foreign recordings not commercially available in the UK market.
Address: 54 Regent Street, London W1R 5PJ.
Tel: 0171 878 7900; Fax 0171 878 7950/60;
E-mail: info@ifpi.org

*MECHANICAL COPYRIGHT PROTECTION SOCIETY

MCPS authorises on behalf of its members (composers, authors and publishers of music) use of their work in the UK and abroad by recording companies, film and video companies, background music operators and other recording bodies and individuals as well as in recordings made by radio and television organisations.
Address: Elgar House, 41 Streatham High Road, London SW16 1ER.
Tel: 0181 664 4400; Fax: 0181 769 8792;
E-mail: info@mcps.co.uk; Website: http://www.mcps.co.uk

NEWSPAPER LICENSING AGENCY

The NLA was established in 1996. It issues blanket licences to permit the faxing and reprographic copying for internal management purposes, of cuttings from its sponsoring publishers' newspapers. The repertoire includes all English and most Scottish national newspapers and many regional and international titles. Licence extensions are available to allow the electronic distribution and archiving of cuttings.
Address: Lonsdale Gate, Lonsdale Gardens, Tunbridge Wells, Kent TN1 1NL.
Tel: 01892 525273; Fax: 01892 525275;
E-mail: copy@nla.co.uk

*PERFORMING ARTISTS' MEDIA RIGHTS ASSOCIATION

P@MRA collects and distributes royalties to performers who have, in the last 50 years, recorded their work on commercially produced records, CDs or cassettes provided these have been broadcast or played in public since

1 December 1996, the date this new right for performers came into force.
Address: 4th Floor, 80 Borough High Street, London SE1 1LL.
Tel: 0171 378 9720; Fax: 0171 378 9715;
E-mail: members@pamra.org.uk

*PERFORMING RIGHT SOCIETY

PRS administers the performing rights in copyright music on behalf of composers and music publishers both British and foreign. The performing rights are the right to perform music in public either "live" or by mechanical means (e.g. by playing a record or turning on a television set) the right to broadcast music and the right to diffuse music (e.g. by cable television).
Address: 29-33 Berners Street, London W1P 4AA.
Tel: 0171 580 5544; Fax: 0171 306 4455;
E-mail: info@prs.co.uk; Website: http://www.prs.co.uk

PHONOGRAPHIC PERFORMANCE LTD

PPL licenses on behalf of its members, comprising mainly record companies, the public performance, broadcasting and cable programme rights in the main repertoire of sound recordings protected in the UK. PPL also administers on behalf of its members, the right to dub (i.e. to re-record) sound recordings for the purpose of playing or broadcasting the re-recorded music in public.
Address: 1 Upper James Street, London W1R 3HG.
Tel: 0171 534 1000; 0171 534 1111.

*PUBLISHERS LICENSING SOCIETY

Established in 1981, the Publishers Licensing Society has non-exclusive licences from 1500 publishers which allow PLS to include their works in the licences negotiated by the Copyright Licensing Agency. PLS represents a wide range of publishers from the multinationals to the single-title publisher. PLS is responsible for ensuring that the publishers receive their share of the fees collected by CLA.
Address: 5 Dryden Street, Covent Garden, London WC2E 9NW.
Tel: 0171 829 8486; Fax: 0171 829 8488;
E-mail:pls@pls.org.uk

VIDEO PERFORMANCE LIMITED

VPL licenses the public performance, broadcasting and cable distribution rights in music video recordings in the UK.
Address: 1 Upper James Street, London W1R 3HG.
Tel: 0171 534 1000; 0171 534 1000; Fax: 0171 534 1111.

Table II: Organisations not generally engaged in collective licensing

* Member of the British Copyright Council

*ASSOCIATION OF AUTHORS' AGENTS

The Association represents the majority of British agents, who in turn, act in business matters for a large proportion of British authors and their heirs, and many foreign authors also. The Association does not represent writers directly.
Address: c/o Mr John McLaughlin, 1 King's Mews, London WC1N 2JA.
Tel: 0171 242 0958; Fax: 1017 242 2408;
E-mail: john@ctmcl.win-uk.net

*ASSOCIATION OF ILLUSTRATORS

The AOI was established in 1973 to advance and protect illustrators' rights and to encourage professional standards. Its membership includes freelance illustrators, illustration agents, clients, students and lecturers. The AOI provides professional advice for illustrators and presents an annual programme of events.
Address: 1st Floor, 32-28 Saffron Hill, London EC1N 8FH.
Tel: 0171 831 7377; Fax: 0171 831 6277;
E-mail: a-o-illustrators.demon.co.uk; Website: http://www.aoi.co.uk

*ASSOCIATION OF LEARNED AND PROFESSIONAL SOCIETY PUBLISHERS

ALPSP is an association of over 100 British learned and professional organisations engaged in publishing, and individuals with interests in publishing. It exists to promote the development of publishing and the flow of publications of its members.
Address: c/o Prof. B T Donovan, 48 Kelsey Lane, Beckenham, Kent BR3 3NR.
Tel: 0181 658 0459; Fax: 0181 663 3583.

*ASSOCIATION OF PHOTOGRAPHERS

The Association was founded in 1968 as the Association of Fashion, Advertising and Editorial Photographers. It represents the interests of and aims to improve the rights of all professional photographers in the UK, as well as promoting the highest standards of work and practice across the industry.
Address: 81 Leonard Street, London EC2A 4QS
Tel: 0171 739 6669; Fax: 0171 739 8707
E-mail: aop@dircon.co.uk; Website: www.aophoto.co.uk

ASSOCIATION OF PROFESSIONAL COMPOSERS

APC represents British composers working in most fields of music. It exists to further the collective interests of its members and to inform and advise them on professional and artistic matters.

Address: The Penthouse, 4 Brook Street, London, W1Y 1AA.
Tel: 0171 629 4828.

ASSOCIATION OF UNITED RECORDING ARTISTS

AURA is committed to representing, advising and collecting performance income for professional recording artists, performers and studio producers across the full range of their careers. AURA monitors legislative, technical and contractual developments which have an impact on the rights of featured performers.

Address: Flat B, 6 Bravington Road, London W9 3AH.
Tel: 0181 960 4438; Fax: 0181 968 8458;
E-mail: 106276.2056@compuserve.com

BENESH INSTITUTE OF CHOREOLOGY

The Institute exists to protect the interests of dance notators.

Address: 36 Battersea Square, London SW11 3RA.
Tel: 0171 326 8031; Fax: 0171 326 8033;
E-mail: BeneshInstitute@compuserve.com

*BRITISH ACADEMY OF SONGWRITERS, COMPOSERS AND AUTHORS

BASCA represents British writers of songs and light music. It exists to assist both established and aspiring British songwriters with advice, information, guidance and encouragement.

Address: 34 Hanway Street London W1P 9DE.
Tel: 0171 629 0992; Fax: 0171 629 0993;
E-mail: basca@basca.org.uk

*BRITISH ACTORS' EQUITY ASSOCIATION

The Association, known generally as Equity, represents actors and other performers in the theatre and on radio and television. It negotiates with employers and gives legal and professional advice on many matters, including copyright and performers' rights.

Address: Guild House, Upper St Martin's Lane, London WC2B 9EG.
Tel: 0171 370 6000; Fax: 0171 379 7001;
E-mail: info@equity.org.uk

*BRITISH COMPUTER SOCIETY
The Society, founded in 1957 and incorporated by Royal Charter in 1984, is the professional institution for information systems engineering and represents over 30,000 computer practitioners. It is concerned with maintaining and improving technical and ethical standards within the profession, and with the protection of their interests.
Address: 1 Sanford Street, Swindon, Wilts SN1 1HJ.
Tel: 01793 417 417; Fax: 01793 480 270;
E-mail: bcshq@bcs.org.uk; Website: http://www.bcs.org.uk

*BRITISH INSTITUTE OF PROFESSIONAL PHOTOGRAPHY
The BIPP represents approximately 4,000 practising photographers in the UK and is the principal qualifying organisation for professional photographers. It looks after the interests of professional photographers generally at all levels.
Address: Fox Talbot House, Amwell End, Ware, Herts SG12 9HN.
Tel: 01920 464 011; Fax: 01920 487 056;
E-mail: bipp@compuserve.com; Website: http://www.bipp.com

BRITISH MUSIC RIGHTS
BMR was founded in 1996. It is the representative body of British music songwriters, composers and publishers. Its members are the Alliance of Composer Organisations, (BASCA, APC and the Composers' Guild), the Music Publishers' Association, the Mechanical-Copyright Protection Society, and the Performing Right Society. British Music Rights promotes British music to the public and to government, is involved in education and training programmes and provides an information service about music as an economic and creative force.
Address: British Music House, 26 Berners Street, London W1P 4AA.
Tel: 0171 306 4446; Fax: 0171 306 4449;
E-mail: british.music.rights@dial.pipex.com

BRITISH PHONOGRAPHIC INDUSTRY LTD
BPI's principal function is to represent the interests in the United Kingdom of the UK record industry.
Address: 25 Savile Row, London W1X 1AA.
Tel: 0171 287 4422; Fax: 0171 287 2252;
E-mail: general@bpi.co.uk; Website: http://www.bpi.co.uk

*BROADCASTING ENTERTAINMENT CINEMATOGRAPH & THEATRE UNION
BECTU protects and improves the conditions of workers in broadcasting, films, cinemas, theatres and other fields of entertainment; and regulates their

relations with employers in collaboration with other trade unions within the entertainment and communication industries. BECTU has more than 30,000 members, many of which have copyright interests, such as directors, writers, production designers and visual artists, etc. Membership is open to all who work in the appropriate industries.

Address: 111 Wardour Street, London W1V 4AY.
Tel: 0171 437 8506; Fax: 0171 437 8268;
E-mail: bectu@geo2.poptel.org.uk; Website: http://www.bectu.org.uk

BUSINESS SOFTWARE ALLIANCE
BSA is a worldwide organisation devoted to eradicating the illegal copying of software, often referred to as "software piracy".
Address: 79 Knightsbridge, London SW1X 7RB.
Tel: 0171 245 0304; Fax: 0171 245 0310;
E-mail: bsa/europe.org.uk

*CHARTERED INSTITUTE OF JOURNALISTS
The CIoJ is both a Chartered professional body and a fully certified, independent trade union. It represents, advises and safeguards newspaper and magazine journalists, radio and television broadcasters, freelances, PR practitioners, workers in multimedia, Internet and other electronic publishing, and others in related fields. It received the Royal Charter in 1890.
Address: 2 Dock Offices, Surrey Quays Road, London SE16 2XU.
Tel: 0171 252 1187; Fax: 0171 232 2302;
E-mail: cioj@dircon.co.uk; Website: http://www.coij.dircon.co.uk/

*CHARTERED SOCIETY OF DESIGNERS
The Society is the representative professional association for designers working for industry and commerce in private practice, public companies or salaried employment. It is the only organisation in the UK to cover all areas of design. It received its Royal Charter in 1976.
Address: 1st Floor, 32-38 Saffron Hill, London EC1N 8FH.
Tel: 0171 831 9777; Fax: 0171 831 6277;
E-mail: csd@csd.org.uk; Website: www.designweb.co.uk/csd

*COMPOSERS' GUILD OF GREAT BRITAIN
The Guild was formed to represent and protect the interests of composers of music in the UK and to advise and assist its members on problems connected with their work.
Address: The Penthouse, 4 Brook Street, Mayfair , London W1Y 1AA.
Tel: 0171 629 0886; Fax: 0171 629 0993.

DIRECTORS' & PRODUCERS' RIGHTS SOCIETY

The DPRS, the collecting society representing British film and television directors, currently administers authorial rights payments on behalf of members under arrangements with foreign collecting socities and in respect of cable re–transmissions, private copying and video rentals. As a resultt of the Copyright and Related Rights Regulations 1996, directors have assigned their right to equitable renumeration for the rental of their work to the DPRS. As yet, the DPRS is not a licensing society.

Address: 15-19 Great Titchfield Street, London W1P 7FB.
Tel: 0171 631 1077; Fax; 0171 631 1019;
E-mail; dprs@dial.pipex.com

FEDERATION AGAINST COPYRIGHT THEFT

FACT enforces rights in UK films and other products by seeking and collecting evidence of piracy and bringing legal (usually criminal) proceedings against infringers.

Address: 7 Victory Business Centre, Worton Road, Isleworth, Middlesex TW7 6ER.
Tel: 0181 568 6646; Fax: 0181 560 6364.

FEDERATION AGAINST SOFTWARE THEFT

FAST enforces rights in computer programs by seeking and collecting evidence of piracy and bringing legal (usually criminal) proceedings against infringers.

Address: 1 Kingfisher Court, Farnham Road, Slough, Berks SL2 1JF.
Tel: 01753 527 999; Fax: 01753 532 100;
E-mail: fast@fast.org; Website: http://www.fast.org.uk

*INTERNATIONAL MANAGERS FORUM

IMF was created in 1992 to represent the interests of Artist Managers in the music business. It has arms in the US, Australia, Canada, Japan and all over Europe. The IMF provides training and educational courses to both its members and other companies in the music business. It has contacts at both Government and Local Government levels and its membership currently stands at approximately 500.

Address: 134 Lots Road, Chelsea, London SW10 0RJ.
Tel: 0171 352 4564; Fax: 0171 351 3117;
E-mail: 101740.2303@compuserve.com; Website: http://www.inf-uk.org

*INTERNATIONAL PEN (ENGLISH CENTRE)

English PEN (Poets, Essayists, Editors, Novelists) is one of the 137 centres which together constitute International PEN - a world-wide, non-political association of writers working for freedom of expression and against

repressive regimes of whatever ideology. PEN is open to any writer, poet, editor or translator actively engaged in any branch of literature.
Address: 7 Dilke Street, London SW3 4JE.
Tel: 0171 352 6303; Fax: 0171 351 0220.

MOTION PICTURE EXPORT ASSOCIATION OF AMERICA
The Association represents the interests in Europe of the US film industry.
Address: Paramount House (4th Floor), 162-170 Wardour Street, London W1V 4AB.
Tel: 0171 437 1327/8/9; Fax: 0171 437 3730.

*MUSIC PUBLISHERS' ASSOCIATION LTD
The MPA promotes and protects the interests of British music publishers and the writers signed to them. It seeks to promote improvements in copyright and other relevant areas of the law, to keep its members up to date on all matters affecting or of interest to them, and to educate the wider public in the importance and value of copyright.
Address: 18/20 York Buildings, London WC2N 6JU.
Tel: 0171 839 7779; Fax: 0171 839 7776;
E-mail: mpa@mpa.co.uk

*MUSICIANS' UNION
The MU is the representative organisation for professional musicians involved in a wide spectrum of musical activities including performance in all types of ensembles, instrumental teaching, arranging, composing and copying music. It negotiates with employers, promotes and supports music and is active in the field of copyright and performers' rights and protections.
Address: 60/62 Clapham Road, London SW9 0JJ.
Tel: 0171 582 5566; Fax: 0171 582 9805;
E-mail: info@musiciansunion.org.uk;
Website: http://www.musiciansunion.org.uk

NATIONAL ARTISTS ASSOCIATION
NAA is a visual artists' membership organisation, founded and run by artists, which campaigns on behalf of practising artists at a regional, national and international level. It works towards advancing the economic situation, working conditions and professional status of visual artists. The Association promotes codes of practice and contracts for the visual arts, advises member artists of their legal and other rights and campaigns to improve their rights.
Address: 21 Steward Street, Spitalfields, London E1 6AJ.
Tel/Fax: 0171 426 0911;
E-mail: naa@gn.apc.org

*NATIONAL UNION OF JOURNALISTS

The NUJ represents over 32,000 members in newspapers, magazine and book publishing, public relations and broadcasting, plus freelances. It gives legal and professional advice on many matters, including copyright and contracts.

Head office; Acorn House, 314 Gray's Inn Road, London WC1X 8DP.
Tel: 0171 278 7916; Fax: 0171 837 8143;
E-mail: nuj@mcr1.portel.org.uk

*PERIODICAL PUBLISHERS' ASSOCIATION

The PPA's main aim is to promote and protect the magazine and periodical industry in the UK. Members represent 80% of periodicals by circulation.
Address: Queens House, 28 Kingsway, London WC2B 6JR.
Tel: 0171 404 4166; Fax: 0171 404 4167;
E-mail: info1@ppa.co.uk; Website: http://www.ppa.co.uk

*POETRY SOCIETY

The Society is the only national organisation solely dedicated to the promotion of poets and poetry. A registered charity founded in 1909, its many activities include a poetry bookshop and mail order service, regular poetry readings, annual National Poetry Competition, assistance and advice to literature festivals, publications and verse speaking examinations.
Address: 22 Betterton Street, London WC2H 9BU.
Tel: 0171 420 9880; Fax: 0171 240 4818;
E-mail: poetrysoc@dial.pipex.com; Website: http://www.poetrysoc.com

PRODUCERS ALLIANCE FOR CINEMA AND TELEVISION

The Association represents the interests of United Kingdom producers of film and television programmes.
Address: Gordon House, 10 Greycoat Place, London SW1 1PH.
Tel: 0171 331 6000; Fax: 0171 233 8935;
E-mail: enquiries@pact.co.uk; Website: http://www.pact.co.uk

*PUBLISHERS ASSOCIATION

Founded in 1896, the PA is the national organisation representing British publishers. Its membership embraces some 600 companies.
Address: 1 Kingsway, London WC2B 6XF.
Tel: 0171 565 7474; Fax: 0171 836 4543;
E-mail: mail@publishers.org.uk; Website: http://www.publishers.org.uk

*ROYAL ACADEMY OF ARTS

The Royal Academy was founded in 1768 to promote the 'Arts of Design' through an annual (Summer) exhibition of fine art works of the highest

merit, the running of the oldest art schools (of painting, sculpture and drawing) in the country and, from 1870, loan exhibitions of international reputation. Membership is limited to 50 Academicians and 30 Associates.
Address: Burlington House, Piccadilly, London W1V 0DS.
Tel: 0171 439 7438; Fax: 0171 434 0837.

*ROYAL PHOTOGRAPHIC SOCIETY
The RPS, founded in 1853, exists to promote every aspect of photography. It does so by organising lectures, workshops and other educational activities; by mounting exhibitions; by publications; and by maintaining an outstanding collection of photographic books, images and equipment. Membership is open to all those interested in photography.
Address: The Royal Photographic Society, The Octagon, Milsom Street, Bath BA1 1DN.
Tel: 01225 462841; Fax: 01225 448688;
E-mail: rps@rpsbath.demon.co.uk; Website: http://www.rps.org

*SOCIETY OF AUTHORS
The Society is an independent trade union (not affiliated to the TUC) which exists to promote the interests of authors of literary and dramatic work in all media. It gives its members legal and business advice, including the vetting of contracts. It has specialist groups for translators and for broadcasting, educational, children's and medical writers.
Address: 84 Drayton Gardens, London SW10 9SB.
Tel: 0171 373 6642; Fax: 0171 373 5768;
E-mail: authorsoc@writers.org.uk;
Website: http://www.writers.org.uk/society/index.html

*WRITERS' GUILD OF GREAT BRITAIN
The Guild is the writers' trade union affiliated to the TUC representing writers' interests collectively and individually in film, radio, television, the theatre and publishing. It comprises professional writers in all media united in common concern to improve the conditions under which they work.
Address: 430 Edgware Road, London W2 1EH.
Tel: 0171 723 8074/6; Fax: 0171 706 2413;
E-mail: smy@wggb.demon.co.uk;
Website: http:\\www.writers.org.uk/guild